LIVING IN PEACE

The Psychology of Interpersonal Relations

Gary R. Collins

KEY PUBLISHERS
Wheaton, Illinois

Distributed in Canada by
Home Evangel Books, Ltd. Toronto, Ont.

ISBN Publisher Prefix 0-87801-002-5
Library of Congress Card No. 73-129072

Wheaton, Illinois 60187

Printed in the United States of America

I close my letter with these last words . . .
Live in harmony and peace.
II Corinthians 13:11*

**This particular quotation is taken from the Living New Testament, but throughout the book many other translations are used.*

PREFACE

"The biggest problem in the church today is that Christians can't get along with each other," declared an experienced pastor. His tragic conclusion provided the initial impetus which led to the writing of this book. All too often we waste our energies fighting among ourselves instead of using our strength effectively in service, prayer and worship. Piously, each side is convinced of the necessity to "take a stand" and to "defend the faith." Scripture is freely quoted to support any given position. Personal prejudice triumphs over truth and masquerades as spiritual conviction.

This book has been written as a practical guide to help Christians in their interpersonal relations. By combining the truths of Scripture with some of the findings of modern psychology, I have tried to offer guidelines which might help us to get along better and to get on with the job of being Christ's ambassadors and witnesses.

As this book goes to press, I am grateful for the help which has been given by a number of people. Albert J. Wollen, Jr., Curtis Wennerdahl, and William Hadeen read the manuscript and offered suggestions, many of which have been incorporated into the final draft. A captive class of students at Trinity Evangelical Divinity School, and groups of people in Ohio and Illinois heard some of these ideas and reacted with helpful suggestions. Mrs. John Aker and Mrs. Ronald Gifford efficiently typed the manuscript, and the men at Key Publishers –

especially Richard Wolff and Bob Hawkins – kept urging me to put these ideas on paper. Then, as usual, my wife Julie offered innumerable perceptive comments and kept the children out of my study while I was writing. To all of these people (including the children), I am deeply indebted and most appreciative.

The problem of getting along with people was of concern to me long before I ever thought of writing this book. During my days as a student (when I should have been studying) I often sat with a friend or two, drinking coffee, and talking far into the night. Two of my fellow students, James A. Seely and Harris H. Lloyd, taught me a great deal about smooth interpersonal relations. It is to them that this book is gratefully dedicated.

To

Jim and Harris

TABLE OF CONTENTS

Chapter 1

THE PROBLEM

Why can't people get along with each other? Why is there so much tension between husbands and wives or between parents and children? Why do brothers and sisters clash, or college roommates have trouble getting along? Why do churchmen, club members, and even nations so often show distrust and disagreement? What causes blacks and whites, labor and management, liberals and conservatives, to disagree with each other – and among themselves? Why is there student unrest, violence in the streets, frequent divorce or conflict between nations – all of which stand as monuments to man's inability to get along with his fellows?

These questions would be meaningless if men were robots, all cast from the same mold, all with similar attitudes, opinions and beliefs. If we were created like pre-cut pieces of a jig-saw puzzle, then we might be able to live in peace, interlocked into a pattern of stability. But men are neither robots nor parts of a puzzle. We are unique, changing individuals who differ from one another in our past experiences, aspirations, attitudes, abilities, values and opinions.

We are also social creatures. Men do not live alone on islands, separated by a gulf from their fellow men. We live together, realizing that it is neither good, possible, nor pleasant for us to live alone. And this is at the root of our interpersonal problems. Because we live in close proximity and because each of us is uniquely different from all others, we are often in conflict.

These tensions between men have a way of snowballing. Family fights and church splits, for example, frequently begin with relatively insignificant issues; but minor disagreements can be like the spark igniting a forest fire. Suspicion, distrust, criticism, jealousy, and tension build up to the point where interpersonal harmony becomes almost impossible – even when both sides sincerely want peace.

Of course, this inability to get along with others is not something new. According to one historian, eight thousand peace treaties were signed between 1500 B.C. and A.D. 1860. Each was supposed to insure permanent peace, but each only lasted an average of two years.[1] If we turn to the Bible, we learn that conflict between people began in the garden of Eden, shortly after Adam and Eve had eaten of the forbidden fruit. When accused by God, the first human beings had a disagreement concerning the reasons for their sin (Genesis 3:12-13). Later, the well known strife between the sons of Adam and Eve led to murder, and within a few years, as the world's population multiplied, the earth was "filled with violence" (Genesis 6:11, 13). After the flood, things were better, but only for a while. In Genesis 13 we read about strife between the herdsmen of Abram and Lot; in Genesis 14 we read about war; in Genesis 15 there is a family dispute in Abram's household – and so on through the pages of the Old Testament.

The New Testament pictures very little improvement. The disciples argued among themselves who was to be regarded as the greatest (Luke 22:24). In the early church, Ananias and Sapphira lied to their fellow believers (Acts 5). Soon the Jews were at odds with the Greeks (Acts 6:1) and later there were disputes over doctrine (Acts 15:2, 7). Many times the Apostle Paul comments in his letters on the disunity in the church and appeals for peace. In writing to the Corinthians, he expressed fear of finding "arguments, jealousy, ill-feelings, divided loyalties, slander, whispering, pride and disharmony" (II Corinthians 12:20). Paul himself, prior to the second missionary journey, was involved in a dispute concerning John and Mark. So sharp was the disagreement that Paul and his partner, Barnabas, separated from each other and went their different ways (Acts 15:36-40).

Although the Bible records many cases of dissension, such interpersonal strife is never condoned or overlooked. On the contrary, strife is strongly forbidden. "It is an honor," wrote the wise King Solomon, "for a man to stay out of a fight. Only fools insist on quarreling" (Proverbs 20:3). The Psalmist noted that it is both good and pleasant for men to "dwell together in unity" (Psalm 133:1). Jesus instructed men to "live in peace with one another" (Mark 9:50); Paul warned Timothy not to be quarrelsome, especially over unimportant things (II Timothy 2:14, 24) and in other passages of Scripture men are encouraged to "be of the same mind" (Philippians 4:2; I Peter 3:8), to avoid divisions (I Corinthians 1:10), and to live "in harmony and peace" (Romans 12:18, II Corinthians 13:11).

Yet, how can men who are in conflict ever reach such a lofty goal? As we consider this problem in the following pages, one thing will be clear: there are no easy answers. Complicated problems seldom yield to simple solutions, and the issue of how to bring about harmonious and peaceful living *is* complicated. The problem is worthy of serious consideration, especially by men and women who are followers of Jesus Christ, the Prince of *Peace*.

---

[1]*From Erich Fromm,* The Sane Society *(New York: Rinehart, 1955), p. 4.*

Chapter 2

THE STARTING POINT

Numerous psychologists have written about the problem of interpersonal relations. Early in this century Alfred Adler, who at one time had been a follower and close friend of Freud in Vienna, concluded that man is innately a social creature whose problems arise when he selfishly struggles to gain personal superiority. To solve his interpersonal problems, Adler concluded, man must cultivate a "social interest" which is characterized by co-operation and concern for the needs of others.[1] On this side of the Atlantic, the famous American psychiatrist, Harry Stack Sullivan, developed what he called an "interpersonal theory of psychiatry." Sullivan believed that we are social beings who get along best when we meet each other's needs and help each other to feel secure.[2] More recently psychologist Rollo May has noted that today we live in a "period of transition, when old values are empty and traditional mores no longer viable." This has caused modern man to feel anxious, apathetic, and so insignificant that our interactions with others really represent a struggle to be noticed.[3]

The insights of writers such as these have contributed much to the understanding and improvement of interpersonal relations, but for men to really get along together, we must begin at a much more basic level. We must first consider man's relationships with his Creator, for *people cannot live in real harmony with each other until they are at peace with God.*[4]

Writing in Germany on the eve of the second World War, Dietrich Bonhoeffer observed that

> Among men there is strife. . . . Without Christ there is discord between God and man and between man and man. Christ became the Mediator and made peace with God and among men. Without Christ we should not know God, we could not call upon Him, nor come to Him. But without Christ we also would not know our brother, nor could we come to him. The way is blocked by our own ego. Christ opened up the way to God and to our brother. Now Christians can live with one another in peace; they can love and serve one another; they can become one. But they can continue to do so only by way of Jesus Christ. Only in Jesus Christ are we one, only through Him are we bound together.[5]

Our first reaction to this statement could be one of disagreement. Indeed there appears to be considerable evidence to contradict Bonhoeffer's conclusion. We all know of non-Christians who get along very well with other people, and of believers who rather than being "bound together," are instead split apart into denominations and feuding factions.

It cannot be denied that non-believers often interact smoothly with each other. Man's very survival depends on a minimum of cooperation and most of us have discovered that we are happier and less anxious if we can learn to live in harmony with others. Because of their upbringing, earlier experiences, personality characteristics, and values, a few men come close to reaching this goal. But even these people often recognize that there is something missing and countless men today feel lonely, insignificant, incomplete, and without meaning in life.[6] Thus, in spite of his best efforts, man by himself can only approach the goal of harmonious living, and although some come closer to reaching it than others, all are frustrated in their efforts.

The lack of harmony among many churchmen can be explained primarily in two ways: some people are church members but are not believers in Christ while others are believers but are not really committed to Christ.

According to the Bible (I Corinthians 2:14; 3:3), people can be classified into three categories: natural, carnal and spiritual men. The *natural man* is the non-believer. While he may know about the Biblical concept of salvation, he considers it foolish and refuses to accept it. His life may be filled with many interests and activities, but there is no place for Christ (see Fig. 2-1). Such men control their own lives. They follow their personal inclinations and as a result, complaining, criticism, jealousy, envy, pride, anger and even hatred characterize their lives. Often they engage in fighting and occasionally they even resort to violence in an attempt to get the best for themselves (Galatians 5:19-21). Such men cannot expect to get along well with others; their very nature leads to strife and tension. Some reach for a high ethical plane, but in spite of admirable qualities all are really sinners (Romans 3:23). Even the best are like wolves in sheep's clothing, because they are enslaved.

Figure 2-1. **The Natural Man.** Life is composed of many interests and activities (represented by the shapes), but Christ (represented by the cross) is outside. This man is controlled by self (s).

Indeed, "there is no one so much a slave as the person who has had his own way all his life. The one who lives under his own authority has a life no larger than himself."[7]

Unlike the natural man, the *carnal man* has recognized his sinful alienation from God. Having confessed his sin and invited Christ into his life, such a man is counted among the believers and referred to as one of the "brethren" (Romans 10:9; I Corinthians 3:1). But the carnal man does not have a satisfying Christian life for he is spiritually immature. His life is characterized by struggle and frustration. He wants to be good but he cannot. He tries to avoid evil, but falls into temptations (I Corinthians 3:3; Romans 7:15-24).

Even though he professes to believe in Christ, the carnal man refuses to submit to God's will and wants, instead, to have his own way (Romans 8:7; I Corinthians 3:3). Christ is part of his life, but not in control (see Fig. 2-2). As a result, the carnal man shows many characteristics of the non-believer, including envy, strife, and divisions (I Corinthians 3:3). Like the natural man, he who is carnal must expect to have trouble in getting along with people. When the churches are filled with carnal Christians – even as when there are non-believers in the church – there is sure to be tension and interpersonal friction.

The *spiritual man* has accepted Christ as Lord and Savior (see Fig. 2-3). There is conscious submission to God and activities stand under divine control. The things of God become more meaningful (I Corinthians

Figure 2-2. **The Carnal Man.** Life is still composed of many interests and activities (represented by shapes). Christ (represented by the cross) is part of life, but he is not in control. Man is still controlled by self.

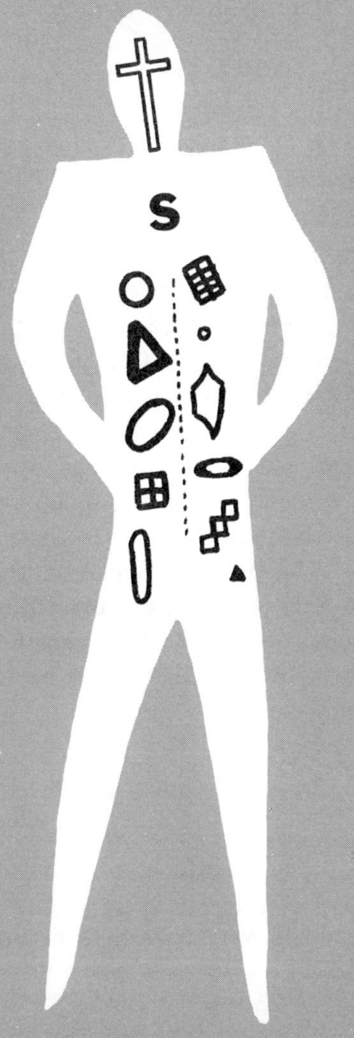

Figure 2-3. **The Spiritual Man.** Life is composed of many activities and interests (some of which are new) but all are under the Lordship of Christ. Man joyfully submits his life to Christ's control.

2:15-16) and the believer's life is characterized by love, peace, patience and gentleness (Galatians 5:22, 23) – all of which increase our ability to get along with others.

The Bible never speaks of natural or carnal men experiencing interpersonal harmony. When the host of angels sang in the presence of the shepherds on the first Christmas night, their message – according to the best Greek texts – was "Glory to God in the highest and on earth *peace among men in whom He is well pleased.*"[8] God is not pleased with men who are non-believers; nor is He pleased with Christians who practically ignore God. There can only be peace and harmony among men who are "one" because they are "in Christ Jesus" (Galatians 3:28). This was Bonhoeffer's conclusion as he watched the Nazi menace creep over Europe. This was the conclusion of the apostle Paul who, writing under divine inspiration, realized that Christ alone brings peace in place of dissension.

> Never forget that once you were heathen, and . . . that in those days you were living utterly apart from Christ. . . . You were lost, without God, without hope.
>
> But now you belong to Christ Jesus, and though you once were far away from God, now you have been brought very near to Him because of what Jesus Christ has done for you with His blood. For Christ Himself is our way of peace. He has made peace between us Jews and you Gentiles by making us all one Family, breaking down the wall of contempt that used to separate us.
>
> By His death He ended the angry resentment between us. . . . He took the two groups that had

> been opposed to each other and made them parts of Himself; thus He fused us together to become one new person, and at last there was peace. As parts of the same body, our anger against each other has disappeared, for both of us have been reconciled to God. And so the feud ended at last at the cross (Ephesians 2:11-16).

Peace, love, and harmony between men do not come because concerned people carry signs encouraging us to "Make love, not war." As noble as the motives of these marchers appear to be, they have started in the wrong place. Man does not attain peace by his own efforts. He starts with submission to Christ. When men are controlled by the Holy Spirit, they are able to love as Christ loved (Galatians 5:22; John 15:12). They may not agree with all other men (Christ didn't), but they will be "very patient and kind, never jealous or envious, never boastful or proud, never haughty or selfish or rude." The love that will come from submission to Christ "does not demand its own way. It is not irritable or touchy. It does not hold grudges and will hardly even notice when others do it wrong. It is never glad about injustice, but rejoices whenever truth wins out" (I Corinthians 13:4-6).

The starting point for peace and harmony is submission to the Lordship of Christ. If we are unwilling to take this step, our relationships with others can at best only be strained and incomplete.

---

[1]*Alfred Adler,* What Life Should Mean to You *(New York: Grosset and Dunlap, 1931).*

[2] *Patrick Mullahy,* Oedipus Myth and Complex: A Review of Psychoanalytic Theory *(New York: Grove Press, 1955), p. 313.*

[3] *Rollo May,* Psychology and the Human Dilemma (*Princeton, New Jersey: Van Nostrand, 1967*), *p. 254.*

[4] *It is doubtless of significance that when God gave the ten commandments, the first five dealt with man's relationships to his Creator. Only then did God give commandments dealing with relationships between men.*

[5] *Dietrich Bonhoeffer,* Life Together (*London: SCM Press, 1954*), *pp. 13-14.*

[6] *These views are expressed by writers such as David J. Riesmann,* The Lonely Crowd (*New Haven, Conn.: Yale University Press, 1950*); *Rollo May,* op. cit.; *Abraham Maslow,* Toward a Psychology of Being (*2d ed.*), (*Princeton: Van Nostrand, 1968*); *and Viktor E. Frankl,* Man's Secret for Meaning (*New York: Washington Square Press*), *1963.*

[7] *Myron Augsburger,* Faith for a Secular World *(Waco, Texas: Word), 1968.*

[8] *See Herschel H. Hobbs,* An Exposition of the Gospel of Luke (*Grand Rapids, Michigan: Baker, 1966*), *p. 53.*

Chapter 3

A LOOK WITHIN

When men are controlled by the Spirit of God do they automatically get along well with each other? If the answer to this question were "yes" there would be no conflict among committed believers and no need for the remainder of this book. It is clear, however, that good interpersonal relationships do not appear spontaneously. Even people whose lives are yielded to the Holy Spirit's control must learn how to get along. If we fail in this task, we can expect to remain immature persons and immature Christians.[1] In order to learn the techniques of harmonious living, we must begin with a long honest look at ourselves.

When people are not getting along very well, there is a strong tendency to blame somebody else for the problems. In many divorce courts and marriage counseling clinics, husbands and wives frequently accuse each other of causing the marital difficulties. Teenagers and parents, on opposite sides of the generation gap, like to blame each other for disagreements and misunderstandings. The same is true when churches split, when labor and management disagree over a contract, when students riot, when wars break out and when truces are violated.

During his ministry on earth, Jesus commented on this tendency to blame someone else for our interpersonal tensions. "Why," He once asked, "do you look at the speck of sawdust in your brother's eye and fail to notice the plank in your own? How can you say to your brother, 'Let me get the speck out of your eye,' when there is a plank in your own? You fraud! Take the plank out of your own eye first, and then you can see clearly enough to remove your brother's speck of dust" (Matthew 7:3-5). On another occasion, Jesus was asked to mediate in a dispute over property. "Master, speak to my brother," was the request, but Jesus spoke instead to the man who was bringing the complaint and told him to check his own attitudes and values (Luke 12:13-15).

To improve interpersonal relations we must not begin by looking at the faults in other people. That can come later. First we must be willing to look within, to see our own faults, and to face the fact that our own behavior may be creating much of the tension (see Acts 20:28 and I Timothy 4:16).

But we do not like to look at ourselves. First, because we are too self-centered to bother and secondly because we are afraid of what an honest self appraisal might reveal. Let us look in more detail at the first of these reasons and leave consideration of the second until the next chapter.

THE SELF-CENTERED WAY OF LIFE

In the Sermon on the Mount, Jesus instructed His followers to seek first the kingdom of God and His righteousness (Matthew 6:33). In the *Living Gospels* account, this passage reads "give Him first place in your life." While many people might agree with the wisdom of this advice, very few are willing to heed it and obey. Most of us are much more concerned with building our own personal kingdoms. We are "seeking first" such goals as success, prestige or security.

This is not really surprising when we consider that our whole society encourages people to be self-centered. During my college days, I was a member of the Navy Reserve. When we began summer training as cadets we were told repeatedly to "always watch out for number one – yourself." In the competitive and demanding life of an officer training program, this was perhaps good advice. With no overseeing parents, concerned Sunday school teachers, or understanding deans, we were on our own. It was every man for himself; some survived the training program, some did not.

Regretfully, this "watch-out-for-number-one" philosophy has become our national way of life. Our self-centered values can be summed up in such phrases as "lay up for yourselves treasures on earth"; "eat, drink, and be merry – for who knows what will happen tomorrow"; "seek the good life, because you can't take it with you"; "tune in, turn on, and drop out" into a world of "experience"; "if you don't blow your own horn, nobody will"; or "grab all the gusto you can get." We hear a great deal about student power, black power, and flower power, and while these are very different, for the most part they all are attempts by minorities to demand self-centered "rights."

This self-centered attitude is something which society encourages from the very beginning of life. We tell our children to be concerned about others but we show them that self-centered competition is more characteristic of our way of living. Before they can babble or crawl, infants are compared with others, so that parents can gloat over the superiority of *their* children. Soon the child learns to compete on his own, first with brothers or sisters and later with the kids in school or with the stars in the Little League. Slowly, children learn that we live in a culture where students compete for grades, athletes compete for attainment and honors, politicians compete for votes, merchants compete for sales, employees compete for promotions and even churches compete for members or "decisions." To survive in this society all of us must compete to at least some extent; and it cannot be denied that as a motivator, competition has contributed much to man's technological and personal achievements. But this competition also encourages us to be self-centered, to be overly concerned about our own personal rights or accomplishments, and to be unwilling to face those issues in our lives which hinder smooth interpersonal relations.

Although I know of no experimental research to support this conclusion, it would seem logical to assume that people who are self-centered are also uninvolved with others and have a tendency to manipulate others. Since all of us are more or less self-centered, we are – in greater or lesser degree – uninvolved and manipulating.

Lack of Involvement

Almost everybody has heard about Kitty Genovese, the young lady who was attacked several years ago as she returned to her apartment late at night. Thirty-eight people watched from their windows in rapt fascination as the girl was beaten for half an hour until she died. Not one of the thirty-eight so much as called the police.[2]

Less familiar is the case of Andrew Mormille, a seventeen-year-old who was stabbed in the stomach while riding on a subway. Eleven riders watched the stabbing, but none came to assist the dying boy even after his attackers had fled and the train had pulled out of the station. Less dramatic, but equally shocking is the experience of Eleanor Bradley. While shopping on Fifth Avenue in New York, this lady tripped and broke her leg. Dazed and in shock she called for help, but for forty minutes the busy shoppers and business executives walked around her until a taxi-driver finally took her to a hospital.

Recently a couple of psychologists[3] tried to find out why people – like Kitty Genovese's neighbors, or the eleven subway riders, or the hurrying throng on Fifth Avenue – fail to help in a crisis. Why is it, they wondered, that car accidents, fires, drownings, attempted suicides, and other crisis situations draw great numbers of onlookers, who stare in fascination but frequently do nothing to help the victims? The research of these psychologists demonstrated that before a person will intervene, he must do three things. These are illustrated in Figure 3-1.

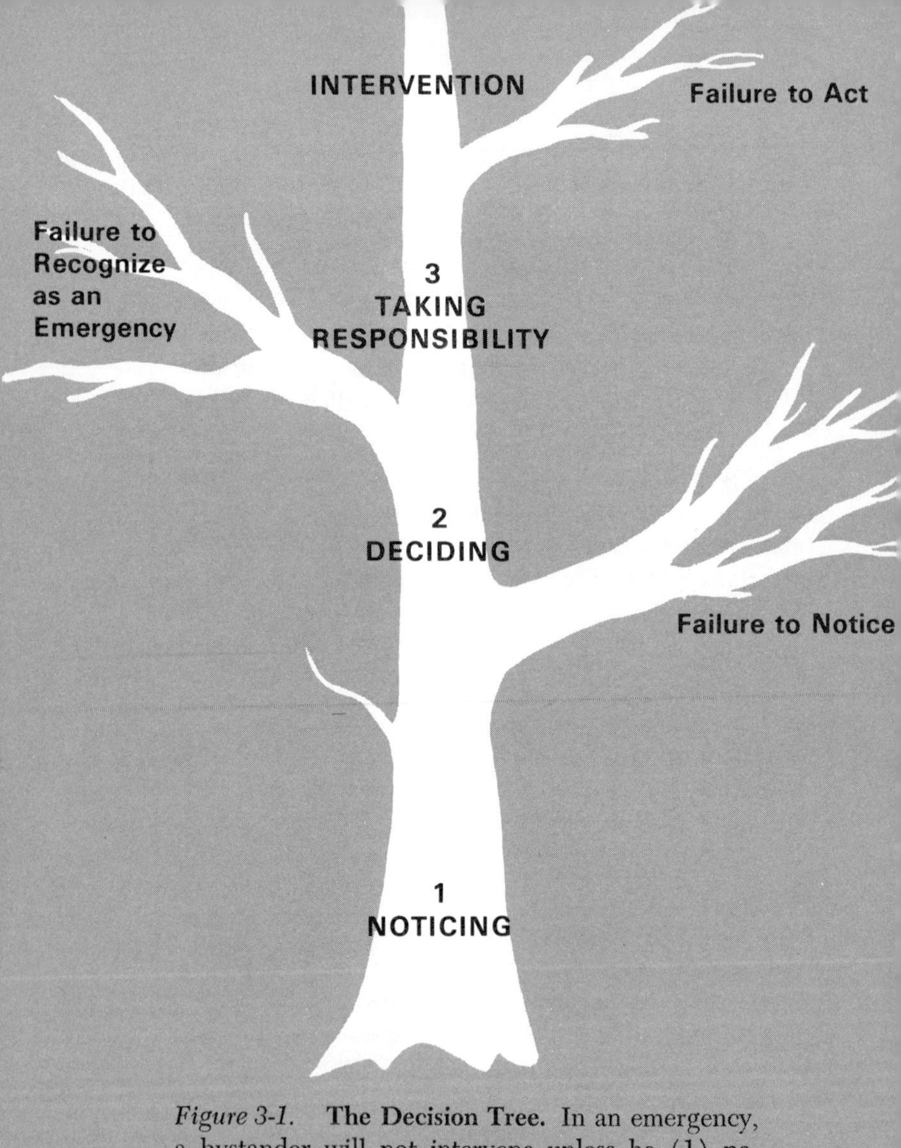

INTERVENTION

Failure to Act

Failure to Recognize as an Emergency

3
TAKING RESPONSIBILITY

2
DECIDING

Failure to Notice

1
NOTICING

Figure 3-1. **The Decision Tree.** In an emergency, a bystander will not intervene unless he (1) notices that something is happening, (2) decides that this is an emergency, and (3) takes personal responsibility for doing something. Adapted from John M. Darley and Bibb Latané, "When will people help in a Crisis?" *Psychology Today*, December 1968. Used by permission.

First, the onlooker must notice that something is happening. The event "has to break into his thinking and intrude itself on his conscious mind. He must tear himself away from his private thoughts and pay attention to the unusual event."[4] In spite of our curiosity at accident scenes, we have learned that it is bad to stare. Caught up in self-centered activity, we often fail to notice when someone else is in distress. Perhaps many of the busy people on Fifth Avenue didn't even see Eleanor Bradley.

But even when a situation is noticed people will not intervene unless they decide that this is in fact an emergency. If they conclude that the situation is *not* an emergency, they will go on their way without getting involved. No one else was helping Eleanor Bradley so perhaps many of those who noticed her assumed that she was drunk or for some other reason not in need of any help.

> A crowd can thus force inaction on its members by implying, through passivity and apparent indifference, that an event is not an emergency. Any individual in such a crowd is uncomfortably aware that he'll look like a fool if he behaves as though it were — and in these cricumstances, until someone aids, no one will.[5]

When an event is noticed and perceived as an emergency, the bystander must make a third decision before acting. He must decide that action is *his* responsibility. Kitty Genovese's neighbors all assumed that somebody else had called the police. As a result, nobody acted and the police were not summoned until it was too late. Presumably when many people witness a crisis, there is less likelihood that any one person will act, since all assume that somebody else will take the responsibility. So hundreds of people left Eleanor Bradley writhing on the sidewalk.

Why do people take no action even when they notice an emergency? It may be that they don't know what to do in order to help.[6] It may be that they are paralyzed by the stress of the situation. It is also possible, however, that they are too self-centered to get involved. Could it be that modern men are so busy with their selfish activities that they prefer to mind their own business and "let the rest of the world go by"?

Even in the church, people are self-centered. Missionaries and other speakers talk of the needs abroad and at home but apparently we fail to take notice, decide that there really is no emergency, or conclude that it is the "full-time Christian worker" – not I – who should take responsibility for witnessing and alleviating the needs of men. With righteous indignation we read in the Bible about the priest and the Levite who "passed by on the other side" and ignored a man in need. We laud the "good Samaritan," who helped, but we are too self-centered to get involved (Luke 10:30-37).

Recently a couple of musicians named Simon and Garfunkel produced a recording which quickly rose to the number one spot on the "hit parade."

When you're weary, in tears, or down and out, the lyrics proclaim, I will comfort you. If you need a friend,

I will ease your mind "like a bridge over troubled water."[7]

In any age, popular music gives a good indication of the thinking of young people and today a new generation is showing increased concern for others. There is a new interest and involvement in social action. This concern must also characterize the followers of Christ. We have no justification for "passing by" unconcerned. Instead, we must respond to the Master's instruction to look at the good Samaritan and "go and do likewise" (Luke 10: 37).

Manipulating Human Behavior

Self-centered people are not only uninvolved, they are also manipulators. Thousands of people have learned "how to win friends and *influence* people," and thousands more have learned that they can boost their own sense of superiority by manipulating the behavior of others.

Of course not all behavior manipulation is bad; some is desirable and quite necessary. Parents and teachers, for example, are often involved in manipulating the behavior of children in ways that will teach the young how to act in a socially appropriate manner. But in spite of this, much manipulation is bad. It is dishonest and disrespectful since it treats other people as impersonal objects.[8] It may give a feeling of superiority to the manipulator but it also contributes to his self-centered way of thinking and hinders his smooth interpersonal relations with others. Furthermore, it interferes with spiritual growth, for when we manipulate others to achieve our own ends, we are building our personal kingdoms and ignore the kingdom of God.

Manipulators tend to be of two kinds: active and passive.[9] The *active* manipulator boldly pulls rank and pushes people around, trying to control others by outsmarting them, by "wheeling and dealing," or by making others feel obligated. Often he sees life as a battle where the goal is to win over all real and potential competitors. In contrast, the *passive* manipulator controls people by pretending to be helpless, incapable, stupid, or a victim of cruel fate. Sometimes he appears to be indifferent, with a "do-what-you-want, I-don't-care" attitude, and at other times he may say "poor-little-me"[10] and play on the sympathy of others. These passive techniques are every bit as effective as active manipulation. By making others feel guilt or sympathy, the passive manipulator subtly uses people to gain his own self-centered ends. As most of this manipulation is unconscious, we aren't even aware of what we are doing, but we are using people, nevertheless.

It would be nice if we could convince ourselves that manipulation is confined to unethical business men or neurotics, but such is not the case. Even "clean-cut" college students manipulate their roommates and, alas, their professors; husbands manipulate their wives, and vice versa; friends manipulate each other; and within the church there are frequent attempts to actively and passively manipulate others in order to achieve selfish ends.

Manipulation in the church occurs on both sides of the pulpit.[10] The church member, for example, can control others by:

– cancelling his pledge and refusing to support the church program;
– cutting off attendance ("If you don't do it my way, I won't come");
– stirring up unrest, by such techniques as gossip or insinuations;
– controlling the curriculum (so that youth groups, for example, are not permitted to even discuss their real problems);
– closing his mind so that he refuses to listen to those with other opinions;
– using cynical clichés (such as "Don't you think we should stick with the Bible, Pastor?")
– putting pressure on the minister (by statements such as "How can you leave when the church is thriving?" or "You know I've always been one of your supporters, but . . .").

The minister can manipulate by using some of the above techniques or by trying some of his own. These include:

– threatening to leave;
– reminding people of his special calling and authority;
– stacking committees, when possible, with men whom he favors (and who, in turn, favor him); or
– reminding people of his special training and skills.

> Phrases such as "of course if you were familiar with current theology . . . ," or "but the original Greek says . . . ," can do a great deal to overpower someone with whom the minister disagrees.

All of these techniques can relegate people to the status of objects to be used – even in the church and often unconsciously – to get what we want for ourselves.

The self-centered attitude which is characterized by lack of involvement and manipulation of others, is opposed to the teachings of scripture and is a basic cause of interpersonal tensions.

Looking again at the Sermon on the Mount we discover that Jesus gave His followers an other-centered plan of living. Be characterized by good works, He said (Matthew 5:16). "If a friend has something against you, apologize and be reconciled to him" (Matthew 5:24). Christians, Jesus said, must give to those who want to borrow (Matthew 5:42) and we should even love our enemies and pray for them (Matthew 5:44). In dealing with others we must be humble (Matthew 5:5), forgiving (Matthew 6:15), nonjudgmental (Matthew 7:1), not concerned with building our personal wealth (Matthew 6:19); but seek instead to live by the golden rule of doing to others what we would like them to do to us (Matthew 7:12). Later in his ministry, Jesus summarized all of this in response to a question from one of his critics.

> Thou shalt love the Lord thy God with all thy heart, and with all thy soul, and with all thy mind.

This is the first and great commandment. And the second is like unto it, Thou shalt love thy neighbour as thyself (Matthew 22:37-39).

Even committed Spirit-controlled Christians are reluctant to try a way of life which involves loving others as we love ourselves. Too often we refuse to look within and will not acknowledge our self-centered characteristics. Nevertheless, until we are willing to take this inward look and until we seek the Holy Spirit's guidance in living an other-centered life, we will continue to have difficulty getting along with our fellow man.

---

[1]*Robert Ekeland,* Are You Getting Half a Bible? Eternity *(November, 1969), p. 21.*

[2]*A. M. Rosenthal,* Thirty-Eight Witnesses *(New York: McGraw-Hill, 1964).*

[3]*Bibb Latané and John M. Darley,* The Unresponsive Bystander – Why Doesn't He Help? *(New York: Appleton-Century-Crafts, 1970).*

[4]*John M. Darley and Bibb Latané,* "When Will People Help in a Crisis?" Psychology Today *(December, 1968,) 2, p. 56.*

[5]*Ibid., p. 57.*

[6]*Ibid.*

[7]*Illustrations could be multiplied.*

[8]*In* I and Thou *(New York: Charles Scribner's Sons, 1958) Martin Buber refers to our tendency to refer to others as an impersonal "it" rather than a personal "thou."*

[9]*Much of the following discussion is taken from Everett L. Shostrom,* Man, the Manipulator, *(Nashville: Abingdon Press, 1967).*

[10]*See Eric Berne,* Games People Play *(New York: Grove Press, 1964).*

[11]*Much of the following discussion is adapted from Macie D. Durnam, Gary J. Herbertson, and Everett L. Shostrom,* The Manipulator and the Church *(Nashville: Abingdon Press, 1968).*

Chapter 4

THE GREAT COVER-UP

As they grow into adulthood, most people develop a number of opinions, attitudes, and feelings about themselves. These opinions – which psychologists lump together and call "self-opinions" or "self concept" – develop as a result of our experiences with other people and with objects. The quarterback on a college football team, for example, may think of himself as "a good athlete," because of his past experiences in handling the ball and because of acclaim from fans and sports writers. If he is also popular with the girls, handsome in appearance but failing his biology course, his self concept might include the idea that "I am a good date, but a poor student."

By the time we reach adulthood, each of us has developed a self concept which has many aspects or parts. Portions of our self concept may be positive ("I'm a good mechanic") while other parts may be negative ("but I'm a poor father"). We may like some things about ourselves ("I'm popular with my friends at work") but there are other things that we dislike ("I'm a procrastinator"). Sometimes our views agree with the opinions that others have about us ("I'm good looking") but other parts of our self concept may be held by us alone ("Everyone says I'm intelligent, but I'm really pretty stupid"). Finally, while some parts of our self concept are conscious, other parts may be unconscious. Thus a person may recognize that he is socially outgoing but "way down deep" – perhaps even at an unconscious level – he concludes that he is shy and afraid of people.

For at least three reasons, this idea of a self concept is important if we want to understand and improve interpersonal relations. In the first place, it appears that action is largely determined by the self-image. The "Don Juan" type of young man who believes that he is "God's gift to women" will act accordingly when he meets members of the opposite sex. The girls may think that he is a conceited pest, but this may have little bearing on his behavior. Similarly the college girl who believes that she "just can't do math" is unlikely to do well in a calculus course – regardless of her real ability or mathematical aptitude. Much of our behavior, therefore, including our interactions with others, is determined by our self concept.

Secondly, we should recognize that the self concept can change, although some parts are easier to change than others. When I moved with my family to a different part of the country, it was not difficult to alter my self concept from "I am a resident of Pennsylvania" to "I am a resident of Illinois." We liked both of these states equally well and living in one place was as acceptable to us as living in the other. When the issue involves an aspect of our self concept which we hold more dearly, however, then the change is slower. Most people find that it takes several months after a wedding to stop thinking "I am single," and to accept the fact that "I am married." Sometimes we resist change altogether. A parent may rigidly persist in his belief that "I am the father of a well-behaved boy" rather than accept the police evidence and acknowledge that he is "the father of a delinquent."

This brings us to a third major conclusion about the self concept: we tend to reveal and emphasize the good while we ignore and hide the bad. Of course there are some who like to dwell on their faults, weaknesses, and deviant behavior; but most of us want to think of ourselves and to have others see us as capable, adequate, desirable people.[1]

Many years ago, Freud discovered that most people keep their weaknesses, faults, selfish urges and socially unacceptable ambitions under cover. We try, often successfully, to hide these characteristics from others and frequently we unconsciously keep them from ourselves. A young man may resent his domineering mother, but it is much more comfortable, and socially acceptable, if he can keep his resentment hidden – even from himself.

Hiding What We Don't Like

In the course of growing up, we learn to use a number of psychological techniques which keep our undesirable impulses under cover and enable us to maintain a positive self concept. Psychologists have tried to identify these "cover-up" techniques and have given them technical names.

"Selective perception" refers to a tendency to see what

we want to see and to ignore the rest. The common observation that "love is blind" refers to the behavior of lovers who often see only what is positive in each other and completely overlook the bad points which are sure to exist. The Don Juan whom we mentioned earlier, might ignore the many sneers and only see the friendly smiles of some kind girls.

Not only are we selective in what we see, but sometimes we are selective in the selection of people with whom we interact. We prefer to choose friends and acquaintances who agree with our self concept, and to ignore those who disagree. An author may write a very poor manuscript, but he need not face this fact as long as he interacts only with the people who agree that he is "a wonderfully talented writer." (Usually one's mother and wife are in this category.) In like manner, a politician who spends time only with his loyal supporters, is able to view himself as being both popular and capable – an opinion which might not be shared by the voters. A somewhat similar technique is used by Christians who have disagreements. Instead of facing issues honestly to determine if we are at fault, we cluster in groups (usually called "factions") and support our positions with selectively chosen Bible verses. Why don't you "love your neighbor"? (Romans 13:9) asks one side, while the other cynically replies that men should control their tongues (James 3).

These examples point to another cover-up technique: the tendency to favorably evaluate those who agree with our self concept and to unfavorably evaluate those who disagree. If a pastor is praised by a board member, the minister may conclude that this is a "perceptive evaluation" in contrast to the "incompetent and unspiritual" rebel who dared to criticize. In response to protests against the Vietnam war, some leading politicians concluded that the protesters were "reckless, impudent snobs," but these were contrasted with a "great" silent majority.

Sometimes we intentionally or unintentionally act in ways which lead other people to behave in accordance with our self perceptions. A female, who considers herself to be sexy, may by her grooming and seductive behavior create this impression in others. A husband who sees himself as considerate, may act in ways which lead his wife and other people to reach the same conclusion.

Of all the techniques which people use to hide what they don't want to face, the "defensive mechanisms" are best known. These are unconscious mental tricks which protect us from anxiety and enable us to maintain our self concept even when there is evidence to the contrary. Psychology textbooks list as many as thirty defensive mechanisms including such tactics as day-dreaming in order to avoid some unpleasant reality; "passing the buck" by blaming others for faults that are really our own; making excuses to explain away our failures; conveniently "forgetting" those things which we don't want to remember; or over-emphasizing our desirable traits so that we can more easily "cover" that which is undesirable.[2]

All of these cover-up techniques are very common

and to some extent necessary. If these defenses were removed, we might be overwhelmed by the inconsistencies in our lives, and inclined to collapse into an abyss of depression and self condemnation. Even people who prefer to see themselves as bad or undesirable use these devices in order to maintain stability and a consistent self concept.

But cover-up techniques are a mixed blessing. They protect us psychologically and help us maintain a consistent self image, but they also blind us and stand in the way of effective interpersonal relations. Just as the self-centered attitude prevents us from honestly looking at ourselves,[3] so these cover-up devices protect us from the painful process of seeing what we are really like. Here is a case where ignorance of ourselves, if it does not bring bliss, at least brings security.

CHARACTERISTICS OF THE "COVER-UP"

Psychological researchers have not yet studied the problem in depth, but it seems that people who are afraid to look at themselves tend to show at least three characteristics: rigidity, an inability to tolerate uncertainty, and dishonesty. These characteristics enable us to keep our self-concept intact so that we don't have to face the possibility that the opinions we hold about ourselves may be wrong.

Rigidity

Most people feel at least a little uncomfortable when they start work at a new job or encounter a novel situation. We are motivated to act appropriately on such occasions, but since the setting is new we cannot be completely sure that our actions will be acceptable. It is for this reason that all of us are somewhat resistant to changes. So long as things are pretty much the same, we can deal with issues by using proven techniques. We know that what has worked in the past will probably work again now and in the future.

When we resist change and tenaciously cling to our long-established ways of doing things, we feel secure. If no demands are made to face new situations, then there is no risk of failure. Our self-concept remains undisturbed since there is nothing to challenge our opinions.

In a complex technological society, however, it requires real effort to ignore change and to rigidly cling to the status quo. Nevertheless, for some people this is preferable to facing the uncertainty of a new job or an untried way of doing things. Afraid that the demands of a novel situation may overtax their resources and puncture their self-concept, such people maintain a rigid resistance to change.

Very often this rigidity is seen in the church. Some members refuse even to consider a change in the Christian education program or in the order of service. Such rigidity is almost always an indication of insecurity but usually this is not recognized. Instead we like to rationalize our inflexible behavior by implying that change, even in minor matters, always represents a departure from the truth of Scripture. Sometimes changes do pull us away from Scripture and should be avoided; but it must be recognized that many of our church traditions have nothing to do with the Bible. The number of meetings and the format of the services, for example, are man-made and therefore open to change. We have a changeless message, but it must be proclaimed to a changing world and this may require periodic variation in techniques. If churchmen are rigid and static in their methods, they can avoid the personal threat of facing something new but they will have difficulty communicating with or getting along with those who are "with it" and secure enough to move with the times.

Intolerance for Ambiguity

This rather fancy psychological term means that some people cannot live with uncertainty. They must see things as either right or wrong, good or bad, black or white. Such people develop an "either-or" attitude: "you are either for me or against me, my friend or my enemy." They feel uncomfortable when there are "shades of gray," and they cannot tolerate periods of uncertainty or indecision.

Probably nobody thoroughly enjoys a state of uncertainty. It is much more pleasant when things are "clear-cut," well defined and organized into neat categories. We like to classify all people into three or four (or more, depending on the theory) concise little groupings. But people can't be fit into pigeon holes. Two opposing political candidates, for example, may have *both* good and bad characteristics. Making a decision may mean that we must choose between alternatives, each with a number of strong points.

For the person who has never really looked at himself, such uncertainty is extremely unpleasant and threatening. He is uncertain how to act when the situation is unclear and afraid of making a mistake. As a result he imposes clearly defined categories where none exist. He decides that all movies are bad, that all Presbyterians are liberal, that all college students are rebels, or that all Republicans are good Christians. This tendency to categorize is, I suspect, at the basis of many interpersonal conflicts. Parents and teenagers, for example, may reach a firm but opposing conclusion about an issue and fail to acknowledge that each viewpoint may have both strengths and weaknesses.

Dishonesty

Even when we are aware of our own attitudes, feelings and impulses, we often keep these hidden from others. It is uncomfortable for us to let people know what we are really like since there is always the danger that people might reject us if they don't like what we reveal. It is safer, therefore, to keep others from knowing us; to use all kinds of "fronts" to convince people that we are different from what we know to be the truth. The strange result of this dishonesty is that we are spared the pain of a further look at ourselves and after a while, we even come to believe our own dishonesty. This was expressed several years ago in the words of a popular song:

Whenever I feel afraid
I hold my head erect
and whistle a happy tune
so no-one will suspect
I'm afraid. . . .
The result of this deception
is very strange to tell
For when I fool the people I fear,
I fool myself as well. . . .[4]

To be honest with ourselves and willing to reveal ourselves to others is of such importance in interpersonal relations that we will discuss it further in chapter 6.

REMOVING THE COVER

The philosopher Socrates once stated that the unexamined life is not worth living. We can never expect to have smooth interpersonal relationships if we refuse to examine ourselves. If we hide from ourselves, how can we expect to be open with others? If I consistently use cover-up tactics and develop personal characteristics to hide what I am really like, how can I sincerely relate to my fellow men?

The Bible encourages self examination (I Corinthians 11:28; II Corinthians 13:5; Galatians 6:3-4) but it is never easy. Our perceptions are often distorted and we all resent facing the truth about ourselves. Therefore, just as we need a good mirror to see what we are like physically, so must we rely on the reactions of other people if we are to understand ourselves psychologically. The opinions and reactions of a warm personal friend can be very helpful in giving us a truer picture of our real selves. This must have been in the mind of Robert Burns when he described the value of coming to see ourselves as others see us!

When a follower of Jesus Christ looks within, he will see faults, inadequacies and perhaps the results of past sin. The inward look, if it is honest, will show us attitudes and values that we would prefer not to see. These may lead us to repentance but should give no cause for discouragement since the inner look will reveal something else. When Christ came into our lives we were transformed into new creatures (II Corinthians 5:17). A fundamental change took place. We received a new governing disposition. Because of Christ we have new potential, new characteristics (Galatians 5:22, 23) and new responsibilities for developing the gifts we have received (Romans 12:3-8; I Corinthians 12). Of course there are individual differences. Some men are more talented than others. Some have greater responsibilities. Some have more scars left from earlier life. But all are followers of Christ and responsible to serve with their God-given capabilities.

Even with the guidance of the Holy Spirit and the help of other people, it is unlikely that we will ever achieve complete self-understanding. Only the Creator can fully know that which is created; but a sincere willingness and honest attempt to look within is an important additional step to improved interpersonal relations.

---

[1]*The self-concept and its influence on behavior is clearly discussed in Arthur W. Combs and Donald Snygg,* Individual Behavior:

A Perceptual Approach to Behavior, *Revised Edition, (New York: Harper & Brothers, 1959).*

[2]*The defensive mechanisms are discussed in most introductory and abnormal psychology textbooks. A good example is James C. Coleman,* Abnormal Psychology and Modern Life, *Third Edition (Chicago: Scott-Foresman, 1964), pp. 96-108. The other cover-up techniques are discussed by Paul F. Secord and Carl W. Backman in* Social Psychology, *(New York: McGraw-Hill, 1964); and in "Personality theory and the problem of stability and change in individual behavior: An interpersonal approach,"* Psychological Review, *(1961), 68, pp. 21-32.*

[3]*See Chapter 3.*

[4]*From* The King and I.

Chapter 5

PREJUDICE

It is unlikely that we ever approach an interpersonal situation with complete neutrality. Usually we have some pre-conceived notions, or prejudgments about the person or persons with whom we will be interacting. This is true even before a blind date or prior to meeting a complete stranger. We often develop tentative ideas about what the other person will be like and when we get together we act accordingly. Even when we are introduced to someone unexpectedly, we quickly "size him up" and jump to some conclusions which affect our behavior.

These prejudgments are frequently based on sketchy and inaccurate information; and often we later discover that the initial impressions and prejudgments were wrong. All of this would be of little importance were it not for the fact that our prejudgments determine both how we *see* other people, and how we *act* towards them. Let us look first at the former.

At any given time, our sense organs are bombarded by a great variety of stimulation. If we were consciously aware of all these sensations, we would probably be overwhelmed and in a perpetual state of confusion. To prevent this, the nervous system "weeds out" a lot of the stimulations and we only notice a few. In writing these words, I am aware of the thoughts I am trying to express; but unless I choose to think about it, or am otherwise aroused, my conscious mind ignores such things as the student voices in the hall, the squeak in my chair, the movements of my chest as I breathe, or the internal signs that tell me it is time for lunch.

This tendency to notice some things and ignore the rest was discussed briefly in the previous chapter. A good example occurred recently when rumors circulated that Paul McCartney of the Beatles died in late 1966 but has been impersonated ever since by a "look-alike." The theory asserted, further, that the remaining three Beatles decided to give out clues of McCartney's death, slipping hints into lyrics and putting signals on the covers of phonograph albums. On the cover of one album, for example, McCartney is wearing both a military medal which is only given to heroes killed in action and a patch with the initials O.P.D. – which is supposed to mean "officially pronounced dead." On another album, McCartney is crossing a street out of step with the other Beatles, and barefoot (the others wear shoes). A car license nearby reads LMW 28 IF. If this number is dialed on a London phone, a recorded voice is reported to give the message "you are on the right track – keep trying." Even the last half of the license plate is thought to be important. McCartney would be 28 IF he had lived to see the album published. While these and other signs may persuade some, most people consider the clues to be ridiculous. McCartney himself says that he is alive; the photographers for the album covers report that the "clues" are of no significance; the OPD looks very much like an arm badge from the Ontario Provincial Police; and in London there is no such telephone number as LMW 28 IF.

All of this illustrates what happens when we accept a premise and then look for evidence to support our case. By selecting facts which are consistent with our conclusions and by overlooking the rest, we can build a case for almost anything.

That selective perception influences interpersonal relations was effectively demonstrated several years ago by some psychologists who were interviewing job applicants. When the applicants arrived for the interview they were told what the interviewer was like. All learned that he was competent, experienced and efficient. In addition, half of the applicants were told that the interviewer was "warm" while the other half were told that he was "cold." The same psychologist interviewed all of the applicants and he did not know beforehand what each had been told. When the interview was completed the applicants were asked "What was Dr. . . . . . . like?" Almost all saw what they had been led to expect, either that he was warm or that he was cold and aloof.[1]

Other research has supported the conclusion that we see in people what we come expecting to see.[2] This is at the basis of prejudice. If we believe that all blacks are lazy, that all politicians are crooks, that all Canadians speak French, or that all women are poor drivers, then we look for these characteristics. If we see them, our prejudice is confirmed. If we fail to find them (which is what will happen in most cases) we pass off our experiences as "exceptions to the rule" and still carry on with our prejudiced attitudes.

Not only do we see in accordance with our expectations, but prejudgments also influence how we act. When we expect people to be hostile, inhospitable, uncooperative, insincere, *we react in accordance with our expectations, even before determining if our expectations are correct.* The story, surely fictional, is told of a man who got a flat tire on a country road. Since he was without a jack, he decided to ask for help in a nearby farm house. On his way, the man started thinking about the occupant of the house. "He doesn't know me, he has no interest in my dilemma, and there is no good reason to think that he will loan me a jack. Indeed, he might conclude that I will steal his jack. Perhaps he won't even trust me in his house and he may even drive me off his property." Just then, the farmer came around the house. "Don't worry!" the motorist exclaimed, "I won't touch your property and I wouldn't be caught dead using your rusty old jack." Defiantly he turned and marched down the road, leaving the bewildered farmer staring in amazement.

Recently, I passed a used car lot which displayed a big sign reading SHY, TIMID SALESMAN ON DUTY. Most of us expect used car salesmen to be anything but shy and timid. Since we expect these men to be aggressive and inclined to use high pressure tactics, we walk on to the lot with our defenses up. If we believed that the salesman was really shy, we would surely act in a very different way. I, for one, didn't believe the sign, (this shows one of my prejudices) but at least it demonstrated that someone in the business had a sense of humor and this in itself might have influenced my dealings with the company had I been in the market for a used car.

WHAT IS PREJUDICE?

Dr. Gordon W. Allport, a famous psychologist who for many years was on the faculty of Harvard University, defined prejudice – somewhat formally – as:

> . . . an antipathy (or dislike) based upon a faulty and inflexible generalization. It may be felt or expressed. It may be directed toward a group as a whole, or toward an individual because he is a member of that group.
>
> The net effect of prejudice, thus defined, is to place the object of prejudice at some disadvantage not merited by his own misconduct.

Usually the term "prejudice" is used to describe generalizations about people of other races or nations, but prejudice is really much broader. We can also make "faulty and inflexible generalizations" about other individuals, members of our own families, political parties, or religious denominations. Consider, for example, the following statements:

– Women are irrational.

– Italians are excitable.

– Bearded students are rebels.

– Jews are crafty businessmen.

– Midwesterners are backward; New Englanders are snobs.
– Baptists are fighters.
– Fundamentalists are rigid.
– The World Council of Churches is unchristian.
– Non-believers have no interest in hearing about Christ.

All of these are prejudgments. While each may be somewhat accurate, none is completely true. Each statement can influence both what we see when we meet members of these groups, and how we will act in the presence of such people. All of the statements are generalizations which, if held rigidly even when there is evidence to the contrary, can hinder effective interpersonal relationships.

DEALING WITH PREJUDICE

There is really nothing wrong with generalizations about people and objects. They enable us to categorize the complex environment in which we live. We talk about "dogs" in general so that we won't have to describe each canine creature individually. By using the term "Quaker" we categorize a group of individuals who share similar religious and perhaps political beliefs. When we conclude that some person is kind, or dishonest, we are summarizing what we have seen in his behavior. In themselves such generalizations are not bad but when they are inflexibly held regardless of facts, they have become harmful prejudices. If we want to get along well with other people, these prejudices must be removed. There are at least three ways in which this can be done.

Recognize the Existence of Prejudice

Awareness is the first step in changing prejudice. When we acknowledge our biased attitudes, we are in a position to do something about them. As I was writing an early draft of this chapter, a salesman called about a product in which I was interested. After listening for a few minutes, I decided that I did not like the salesman and it was only after our conversation had ended that I consciously recognized what had happened. Based on a limited telephone contact, I had made some snap judgments about a man. Later, when he called in person to demonstrate his product I was aware of my attitude and tried to act, not in accordance with my prejudgment, but in light of the new information I was gathering through face to face contact. Because of this, we got along well; many of my initial impressions changed and I was happy to purchase his product.

Recognizing our personal prejudices is rarely this easy, however. Often, people will deny that they are prejudiced even when these pious assertions are contradicted by their behavior. How can we more clearly see our biases? The answer to this question has been anticipated in earlier chapters. When we have increased knowledge about ourselves, we are better able to recognize and alter our biases about others. According to Allport, people who look closely at themselves are more tolerant of others. "People who are self-aware, self-critical, are not given to the ponderous habit of passing blame to others for what is their own responsibility. They know their own capabilities and shortcomings."[4] They have no need to feel greatly superior to others, are less rigid, more secure, and able to tolerate ambiguity.[5] Self insight may not cure prejudice, but it is a necessary step to its elimination.[6]

RECOGNIZE THE ORIGINS OF PREJUDICE

Prejudice arises from two major sources. The first of these is exposure to the attitudes of others. No child is born prejudiced; such beliefs are always acquired. This was expressed succinctly in *South Pacific.* One of the songs says:

> You've got to be taught
> To love and to hate
> Before you are six, or seven, or eight
> To hate all the people your relatives hate
> You've got to be carefully taught.[7]

The child who becomes prejudiced, has learned from the attitudes and behavior of his family, peers, and teachers. He learns from the mass media such as movies, comic strips, magazines, television (notice how often a Latin American is the "bad guy" in cartoons) and even textbooks. We also learn prejudice in church.[8] When we talk about "liberals," "Catholics," "fundamentalists" and even "the world," we are passing stereotypes on to our children.

People can reveal their prejudices, even when nothing is said verbally. Children are especially perceptive and quickly pick up the attitudes of parents and Sunday School teachers. We might tell our children how to act and think, but to use an old cliché, our actions speak louder than our words. In homes which are harsh, suppressive, critical, and threatening, the child is sure to "acquire suspicions, fears, (and) hatreds that sooner or later may fix on minority groups. . . . Parents who *teach* the child specific prejudices are also likely to train the child to develop a prejudiced nature."[9]

The second source of prejudice is personal experience with members or a member of the minority. Contact with a loud-mouthed, boasting, demanding "ugly American" tourist, may easily prejudice a European against all Americans. Riots and disturbances caused by 2% of a college student body may prejudice a state legislature against the whole university. Some people read about the opinions of Bishop Robinson and the late Bishop Pike and conclude that these men represent the views of all Episcopalians. This is what scientists call "generalizing from the particular." We take a small bit of information and apply it to more people than it really fits.

Why should a person generalize from the particular? Why dislike a whole group just because one person offends? If the initial experience with one person is traumatic (if the tourist stole a large sum of money, for example) we can quickly jump to conclusions about a whole group. Likewise, if we are frustrated with life, anxious, guilty, or otherwise distressed, we are likely to unconsciously look for a scapegoat whom we can blame for our troubles. If one person offends us in even minor ways, we easily become prejudiced against the offender and his group.

Work to Reduce Prejudice

Education is one way to reduce prejudice. Since our beliefs about people are often based on incomplete and inaccurate information, we should get more facts. In theory, this sounds logical but in practice it often doesn't work. The prejudiced person doesn't believe the information which is provided. He rejects it as being untrue propaganda, or counteracts it with contradictory "evidence." Try to convince a prejudiced white man that blacks are "good guys" (or vice versa) and the white man will muster evidence to refute you. Try to persuade a frustrated deacon that the pastor is "a reasonable and concerned" man, and your arguments will fall on deaf ears or perhaps be dismissed as irrelevant. Try to tell some experienced pastors that critical church members "really want to see things improve," and you will be ignored.

To reduce prejudice it appears that personal contact is much more effective. Research has shown that prejudice is reduced considerably when children of different races or religions get together at camp, or when soldiers are together in the same fox-hole. Even in these situations, however, prejudice can exist. "That nice young black boy" can be passed off as an exception to the group characteristics. When we rejoin the groups where we learned our prejudices, the old biases often return and are strengthened.

For damaging prejudice to really decline, *we must sincerely want to lose our unproven biases;* we must be willing and secure enough to honestly look at our prejudices. In as unbiased a way as possible, we must learn what we can about the object of our prejudices, and we must be willing to relate on a personal level with the person or persons against whom we are prejudiced.

This is surely the Biblical way. Even if someone has wronged us, there is no scriptural justification for sulking, gossiping, or thinking a lot of hostile thoughts about the other person. Instead, we are instructed to go to the one with whom we disagree and to talk with him *before* telling others about the situation (Matthew 18:15-17).

When Jesus dealt with people He recognized individual differences in education, status, ability and spiritual maturity. He dealt with people in accordance with their level of understanding and sincerity, but He never implied that some people were superior (or inferior) because of their race, nationality or status in life. Christ came to earth as a man because God loved "the world," i.e., all men (John 3:16). God does not see people in accordance with their external circumstances (I Samuel 16:7). When we become believers, we are all one in Christ Jesus. "Gone is the distinction between Jew and Greek, slave and free man, male and female" (Galatians 3:28). Gone is the distinction between the importance of various fields of Christian service. All members are necessary if the body is to function efficiently and none of us should conclude that we are more (or less) important than some other servant of Christ (Romans 12:3-5; I Corinthians 12; Ephesians 4:1-16).

It is not easy to eliminate our prejudices. Indeed, it may be that there is no such thing as a completely unbiased person. We who are followers of Christ must nevertheless learn to recognize our biases and, with His help, seek to eliminate or reduce them. As we do this, we will be increasing our ability to get along with others.

---

[1]*Allen, Bernadene V., Wiens, A. N., Weitman, M., and Saslow, G. Effects of warm-cold sit. on interviewee speech.* Journal of Consulting Psychology, *29, 1965, pp. 480-482.*

[2]*See also S. E. Asch, "Forming Impressions of Personality,"* Journal of Abnormal and Social Psychology, *41, 1946, pp. 258-290, and H. H. Kelley, "The warm-cold variable in first impressions of persons,"* Journal of Personality, *18, 1950, pp. 431-439.*

[3]*Gordon Allport,* The Nature of Prejudice *(Garden City, New York: Doubleday, 1954), p. 10.*

[4]*Ibid., p. 408.*

[5]*Ibid., chapter 27.*

[6]*Ibid., p. 312.*

[7]*From* South Pacific.

[8]*In a controversial study, two sociologists concluded that Christian churches foster anti-semitism in America. See Charles Y. Glock and Rodney Stark,* Christian Beliefs and Anti-Semitism *(New York: Harper & Row, 1966). Allport (op. cit., chapter 28) concludes that the churches create prejudice but they also do much to reduce or eliminate it.*

[9]*Allport, op. cit., p. 283.*

Chapter 6

AWAY MASKS

In this day of Hollywood spectaculars, it is hard to imagine that the actors of ancient Greece simply held up masks to show their roles to the audience. Today, the theatre is much more sophisticated about makeup, and even non-actors can put on realistic "paper faces" at Halloween, masked balls, Mardi Gras celebrations and similar events.

The masks that modern people wear are not all made of paper maché or reserved for festive occasions. Every day, each one of us puts on a number of faces and plays a variety of roles. Beginning in early childhood we learn what is "socially appropriate behavior," acquire culturally approved ways of speaking or acting, and learn what is suitable for our sex, age, and position in life. Much of education is spent in mastering these social norms, learning what is appropriate behavior for the different life situations which we encounter. Such role-playing may seem phony, but unless we do at least some of it, and do it well, society will be in danger of collapse.

It happens very often that we play these roles too well. So capable are people of "putting up fronts" that they hide their real identity. College roommates, church members, fellow employees, and even members of the same family often spend a great deal of time together, but never really get to know each other as persons. "I wish I knew what he is *really* like," is not an isolated comment.

More tragic is the increasing evidence that many modern people are so involved in playing roles that they have lost sight of their own selves. They wonder who am I? What am I really like – way down deep? Why am I here?

As we move into the seventies, a quiet rebellion is taking place. It has hit the college campuses, it has burst into society, and it is creeping into the church. It is a rebellion against the dishonesty, phoniness, and camouflage which keeps people hidden from each other and from themselves. One psychologist has expressed it in this way:

> . . . we have chosen to conceal our authentic being behind various masks. We usually assume that the *other* man is hiding or misrepresenting his real feelings, his intentions, or his past because we generally do so ourselves. We take it for granted that when a man speaks about himself, he is telling more or less than the unvarnished truth as he knows it.
>
> We conceal and camouflage our true being before others to foster a sense of safety, to protect ourselves against unwanted but expected criticism, hurt, or rejection. This protection is purchased at a steep price. When we are not truly known by the other people in our lives, we are misunderstood. When we are not known, even by family and friends, we join the all too numerous "lonely crowd." . . .
>
> A choice that confronts every one of us at every moment is this: Shall we permit our fellow

> men to know us as we now *are,* or shall we seek instead to remain an enigma, an uncertain quantity, wishing to be seen as something we are not?[1]

This question is of concern to Christians and non-believers alike. If we want to get along better with other people, we must be willing to experience a greater honesty not only before others, but before God and before ourselves.

HONESTY BEFORE GOD

When Adam and Eve were in the garden shortly after their sin, they tried unsuccessfully to hide from God by crouching among the trees (Genesis 3:8). Many years later, David concluded that even the dark of night could not hide man from God (Psalm 139:11, 12). "O Lord," he cried, "You . . . know everything about me. . . . I can never get away from God" (Psalm 139:1, 7). Even our secret sins are known to Him (Psalm 90:8).

Most of us have not learned this lesson. Even Christians act as if God periodically looks the other way and is unaware of our sinful thoughts and behavior. The churches are filled with people who, through habit or social pressure, talk and act like committed Christians and pray prayers filled with evangelical clichés, but who are really trying to "fake it" before God. This is deliberate dishonesty. It does not fool God and often does not fool other people. The only person whom we deceive is ourself.

Every believer must learn to be honest before God. We must tell Him frankly about our real feelings, frustrations, and aspirations. Like the psalmist, we must dare to ask God to search us, to know us, to test us, to point out what is wrong with us and to lead us (Psalm 139:24, 25). The alternative is phoniness and a cowardly attempt to hide behind a mask that is transparent. When we refuse to be open before God, it is unlikely that we can really be honest before ourselves and others.

HONESTY BEFORE OURSELVES

In preceding chapters we have tried to show that self-appraisal is biblical. We who believe in Christ must examine ourselves and confess our sins. Periodically we must "check-up" on ourselves to make sure that we are really committed to the Lord and not just pretending (II Corinthians 13:5).

To take a close frank look within is a painful process, certain to reveal sin and characteristics we would prefer to ignore. But if we can be honest enough to make a self-appraisal, we will also become more tolerant, less rigid, and better able to accept the uncertainties of life.[2] This self-examination may also lead to greater emotional stability,[3] and by being honest with ourselves we discover that we are more honest before others.[4]

HONESTY BEFORE OTHERS

Hiding from others is not especially difficult. Men do not possess God's all-powerful ability to see within (I Samuel 16:7) and for this reason it is often possible to deceive others about our real nature. Some have argued persuasively that this deception might even be good. According to Professor Harvey Cox of the Harvard Divinity School, modern man needs to remain at least somewhat anonymous and hidden. In the small towns which characterized America in a bygone era, privacy was impossible. Everyone knew about everybody else and it was pretty difficult to put up a front. By moving to the impersonal "secular city," man has been able to protect himself with a mask of anonymity. He can live in a high-rise apartment or a plush suburb and he need never learn his neighbor's name. Freed from the fishbowl existence of the small town, Cox suggests, men today have more time and energy to develop close relations with a few intimate friends whom they themselves select.[5]

While there is no value and probably no wisdom in exposing ourselves to the whole world, it *is* important for us to be honest before at least a few people. "Every maladjusted person," writes psychologist Sidney Jourard "is a person who has not made himself known . . . to at least one significant other person."[6]

Such honesty before others is consistent with the principles of Scripture. In the book of James (5:16), we are instructed to confess our faults to one another and to pray for each other. The early church was composed of Spirit filled men and women who worshipped God together, shared their possessions and undoubtedly shared of themselves as they met together (Acts 4:31-35). To these Christians, the deception of Ananias and Sapphira was a powerful lesson in the importance of honesty (Acts 5:1-11). In trying to deceive others, the Bible notes,

Ananias and Sapphira were really lying to God (Acts 5: 4).

But can honesty and sharing be overdone? Can we be too open? Very frequently great truths come in pendulum fashion. The philosopher Hegel recognized this many years ago. In our frustration over some undesirable situation, we go too far in the opposite direction before arriving at a more healthy midpoint. Recognizing that our great grandparents were overly rigid in their morals and unwillingness to even mention sex, for example, we swung in the opposite direction and have now become open about the subject to the point of obsession. Frustrated over the extent to which universities are being run by a small group of administrators, some student radicals have moved to the equally undesirable position of demanding that all power be given instead to a small group of militants. The same trend is apparent in the current emphasis on honesty. Appalled by the phoniness and dishonesty of modern man, many are demanding and taking the license to speak obscenities in public and to be brutally honest even if others are thereby hurt. Such a self-centered and intolerant attitude is surely unchristian, disrespectful of the people who are harmed, and probably worse than the phoniness which is so much disliked.

Nowhere is this more clearly seen than in the encounter or T-groups which are literally springing up everywhere. There can be no doubt about the value of such groups. Research studies and the testimonies of countless participants have shown that a revealing of oneself to others is an intensely enriching and psychologically healthy experience.[7] To honestly share with others in a group can be enlightening and, for Christians, spiritually rewarding.

Very often, however, such groups become vicious. In the name of honesty, group participants attack each other with the kindness of wolves attacking a defenseless rabbit. To verbally tear at each other and to strip off one's clothes (as is sometimes done) in an attempt to be authentic before others, is both cruel and immoral. To drop one's defenses is an enthusiastic desire to be fully transparent before all others is foolish and sometimes suicidal.[8] Increased honesty which is good in itself, can be very dangerous if allowed to run rampant.

It is important, therefore, that our honesty be tempered by love. Keith Miller has exprcssed this very clearly. As one of the earliest and most influential advocates of honesty among believers,[9] he warns that he is

> NOT suggesting the starting of some sort of honesty cult. Such groups are often harmful and almost invariably wind up being *un*Christian. The object of honesty . . . is not to reveal immoral and lascivious incidents. The object is rather to begin to acknowledge to God and to each other the true nature of the personal struggles of living in the world today, so that we can begin to find freedom, healing, and forgiveness – and provide a place where others can experience these things. *One does not rip off his mask (or anyone else's).* Rather *he becomes willing for God to remove the unnecessary part of his facade gradually* by providing the security he needs to be more honest. Also a

ground rule in this type of group is never to share something in such a way that it may make *another* person vulnerable. The highest value in the Christian life is not honesty – but love (I Corinthians 13). This is a very important basic difference between Christian joint-adventuring and some (humanistic) psychologically oriented groups.[10]

Honesty tempered with Christian love – this is a balanced guideline. It lets us reveal our true feelings, in an atmosphere where people seek to be characterized by a love which is "patient and kind, never jealous or envious, never boastful nor proud, never haughty nor selfish nor rude . . . not irritable or touchy" (I Corinthians 13: 4, 5).

But honesty must also be balanced with humility. Too often a willingness to reveal oneself becomes cause for self-righteous pride. "Look at me," we say by our attitude if not by our words, "I have so many faults and hangups but I am brave enough to confess everything." Implied is the view that those who don't tell all are really phonies – deceptive people who, because of psychological or spiritual immaturity, are afraid or unwilling to reveal themselves. But it is every bit as hypocritical to confess faults in order to enhance our status, as it is to deceptively pretend that we are spiritual when we are not.

Honesty coupled with love and humility makes for better group discussions and for improved interpersonal relations.[12]

---

[1]*Sidney M. Jourard,* The Transparent Self *(Princeton, New Jersey: Van Nostrand, 1964), p. iii.*

[2]*Gordon W. Allport,* The Nature of Prejudice *(Garden City, New York: Doubleday, 1954), chapter 27.*

[3]*Edward Joseph Shoben, Jr., "The Examined Life as Mental Health"; In O. H. Mowrer, ed.,* Morality and Mental Health, *(Chicago: Rand McNally, 1967), pp. 382-388.*

[4]*Aaron J. Ungersma,* Escape from Phoniness *(Philadelphia: The Westminster Press, 1969), p. 38.*

[5]*Harvey Cox,* The Secular City *(Revised Edition); (New York: Macmillan, 1965).*

[6]*Jourard, op. cit., pp. 26 and 25. See also Sidney M. Jourard, "Healthy Personality and Self Disclosure," in Mowrer, op. cit., pp. 389-395.*

[7]*See Carl Rogers, "The Group Comes of Age,"* Psychology Today; *(December, 1969, 3), pp. 27-31, 58-61.*

[8]*Sidney M. Jourard,* Disclosing Man to Himself, *(Princeton, New Jersey: Van Norstrand, 1968), pp. 47-8.*

[9]*See Keith Miller,* The Taste of New Wine, *(Waco, Texas: Word Books, 1965).*

[10]*Keith Miller,* A Second Touch, *(Waco, Texas: Word Books, 1967), p. 142, Italics added.*

[11]*Joseph M. Tewinkel, "The Cult of Honesty,"* The Alliance Witness, *(January 21, 1970), 105, pp. 4-6.*

[12]*For a layman's introduction to small honesty groups in the church, see Clyde Reid and Bruce Larson, et. al.,* Groups That Work *(Grand Rapids, Michigan: Zondervan, 1967).*

Chapter 7

SEEING ANOTHER'S POINT OF VIEW

In the preceding chapters we have argued that smooth interpersonal relations depend on our relationship to Christ and on our willingness to honestly face ourselves. By understanding – even partially – our own self centered attitudes and prejudices, and by trying to change our behavior, we can better interact with others. When we stop trying to manipulate people selfishly and instead relate to them as individuals, they are more likely to respond favorably to us.

All of this does not hide the fact, however, that interpersonal relations involve more than one person. Other people are also involved, and in our attempts to get along we must look beyond ourselves and learn to see how others view the world.

Every once in a while, some enthusiastic football player grabs the ball in the excitement of a game, and runs the wrong way. To the people in the stands, this is an act of great foolishness, but to the athlete as he runs down the field, his actions are perfectly sensible. Later, when he realizes his mistake, the football player will agree with the evaluation of the fans, but as he is running he is doing what appears to him to be most reasonable and necessary.

This example illustrates a very basic truth about human behavior. The way people act can always be seen from two perspectives: from the point of view of the observer and from the view of the actor. Very often, the person who is acting, and the people who watch, see things from different perspectives. Later, both views of the situation may change, but *at the instant of action* most people do what they think is the most rational and effective thing to do in the situation as they understand it.[1]

If we want to understand and get along with other people we must try to see things from the other's point of view as much as possible. When we fail to accurately perceive the other person, the stage is set for interpersonal conflict. As an example, let us suppose that a young couple are out on their first date together. At the end of the evening they arrive at her doorstep and as she thanks him for the evening, the girl smiles. To her the smile may mean, "I enjoyed being with you." To him the smile may mean, "why don't you kiss me goodnight?" Let us assume (and this does not take much imagination) that the young man acts in accordance with *his* perception and kisses the girl. She may or may not be pleased about this and will act accordingly—perhaps by slapping his face, perhaps by smiling again.

On a first date, there may be misunderstanding and awkward moments because the couple does not know each other well enough. Later, when a man and a woman have been married for many years, they know each other well and can even predict how in a given situation, the other will think and act. Because they understand each other's perceptions, the husband and wife are capable of greater understanding and smoother interpersonal relations.

This is illustrated in figure 7-1. In part A, we see two people, P1 and P2, viewing event X. If P1 and P2 speak the same language, have grown up in the same culture and have had similar past experiences, they are likely to largely agree in their view of X. They see it from a similar perspective and they can readily understand the other's point of view. In part B, however, P3 and P4, perhaps because of different backgrounds or past education, see event X from very different angles. As a result, they may reach different conclusions about X and have trouble communicating.

If X is the war in Vietnam, and P1 and P2 are members of the President's cabinet, there may be considerable agreement, but when a military commander (P3) and a reluctant recruit (P4) view the war, their views may differ considerably. By substituting almost any event or situation for X, we can see how the behavior of people differs because of their divergent views.

For smooth interpersonal relations and effective communication, it is not necessary that we *agree with* each other's position. On the contrary, healthy, respectful disagreement is often desirable and has probably helped man in his progress. But we must try to *see* the other person's view. We must attempt to appreciate his beliefs, values, experiences, hopes and needs. A good place to try this is in the home or the church where personal tensions are often present.

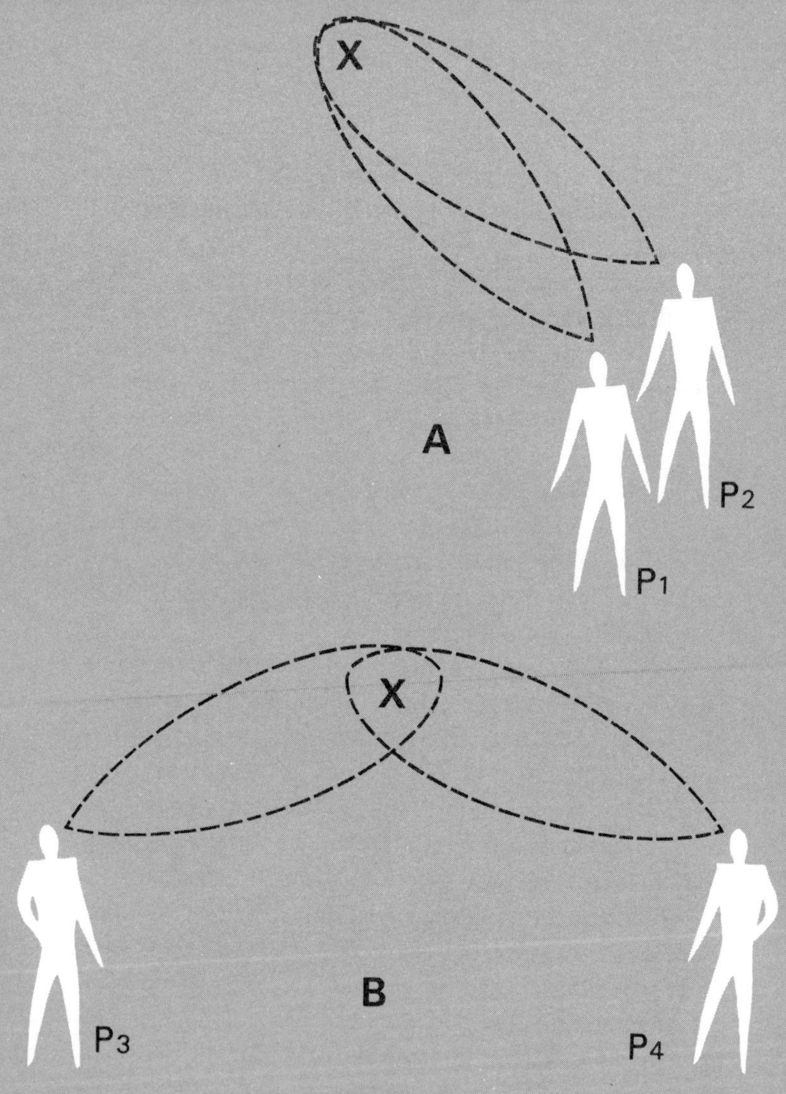

Figure 7-1. **Ways of Viewing Events.** Event or situation X may be viewed by two people who have similar perspectives (A) or by people whose viewpoints may differ substantially (B).

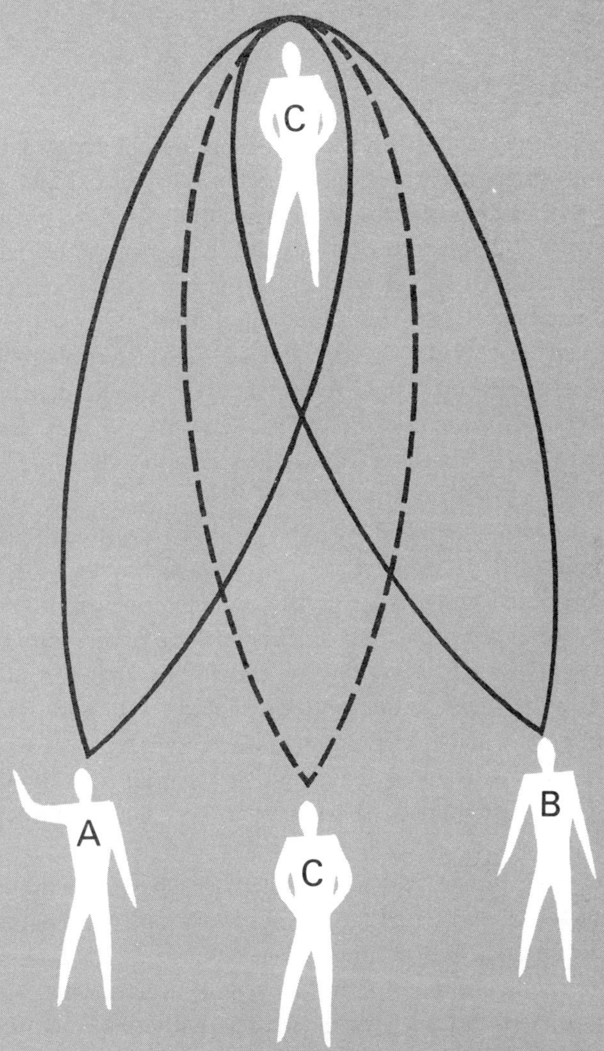

Figure 7-2. **Three Views of One Person.** C may be viewed from A's perspective, from B's perspective, or from the perspective of C himself. Some of these views overlap, others are unique to the viewer.

Before leaving this topic, it must be pointed out that individuals differ not only in their views of external objects and events, but also in their opinions about people. Figure 7-2 illustrates three views of person C. A has a view of C, B has view of C, and C has a set of opinions about himself. In this situation, all three agree on some things about C (see the shaded area), but there are other issues on which A and B agree but C does not. Likewise, there are views held in common only by A and C or by B and C, as well as some opinions held by each of the observers alone.

It is unlikely that two people will ever completely agree in their viewpoints, but the more information we have about an event or person, the more we can learn to appreciate and partially understand the other's point of view. Instead of arguing or concluding that the other person is blind to the facts we should try to understand his perspective. In doing so, we must realize that others, like us, tend to see things in accordance with their personal prejudices, self-concepts, and unique past experiences.

Seeing things from another's perspective is not difficult if, like P1 and P2 of figure 7-1, two people have similar backgrounds and attitudes. On some issues, for example, Christians are able to get along quite well because their basic views are in agreement. The early believers never debated the existence of God, the resurrection of Christ, or the possibility of miracles because everybody accepted the truth of these and similar doctrines.

It is when people approach an issue with different

viewpoints, as in the lower half of figure 7-1, that problems begin to arise.[2] Even the spiritual giants in the early church had differences of opinion (that is, different perspectives) regarding the relationships between Jewish and Gentile Christians. When this happened, they met and discussed their differences, so that they could eventually arrive at a mutual understanding and resolution of the difficulties (Acts 11:1-18; 15:1-31).

The ability to appreciate another's perspective is not an inborn characteristic, nor is it a gift which is bestowed when we become Christians. It is, instead, a skill which is constantly to be learned and perfected. Many people have the false opinion that psychologists can read minds and that they are always analyzing others even at social gatherings. Most professional counselors have at some time seen people laugh nervously and politely excuse themselves from the presence of the supposed mind-reader. While no psychologist has such powers (and it probably would not be good if they did) most counselors *have* become highly skilled and astute in their ability to observe human behavior. The professional counselor has learned through his training and experience to watch people carefully and to appreciate what their behavior means. But this ability is not limited to a few specialists. All of us can increase our skills in this area by observing people and by trying to think and feel as they do. If the check-out girl in the super-market is a little grouchy at five o'clock, put yourself in her shoes and think how you would feel after standing in one spot all day pounding a cash register and handing out green stamps. By understanding her situation, we are better able to appreciate the tired frustration which she may feel, and we can better tolerate her grouchiness.

In all of this we must remember that our understanding will never be perfect. We can see things "as if" we were another person, but we can never completely get into his skin and think from his perspective. Only God can do that. He understands perfectly because He perceives with such accuracy (I Samuel 16:7). Jesus demonstrated repeatedly that He could see people as they really were, even though He did not always like what He saw. He did not, for example, approve of the motives of the religious leaders who tried to trick Him with their questions, but He understood nevertheless – just as He does today.

As we learn to be more perceptive, we who are Christians have the guidance and teaching of the Holy Spirit. Paul acknowledged this in his prayer for the Colossians. "We are asking God," he stated, "that you may see things . . . from his point of view by being given spiritual insight and understanding" (Colossians 1:10). Our little minds can only partially comprehend the viewpoint of God (Romans 11:33) but this helps us to more accurately see others.

To improve our relationships with others we must seek the guidance of the Holy Spirit as we actively work to see objects, events, situations and persons (including ourselves) through the other person's eyes.

---

[1]*Arthur W. Combs and Donald Snygg,* Individual Behavior: A

Perceptual Approach to Behavior (*Revised Edition*); (*New York: Harper and Brothers, 1959), pp. 17-18.*

[2]*In a perceptive little book, an anthropologist suggested several years ago that Americans are "in the stone age of human relations in the overseas field" because they fail to appreciate how people see things in other countries. Totally ignorant of what is expected in other cultures and unaware of how people communicate elsewhere, the well-meaning American frequently insults foreigners who interpret his behavior differently than he intends. See Edward T. Hall,* The Silent Language (*Greenwich, Conn.: Fawcett Publications, 1959*).

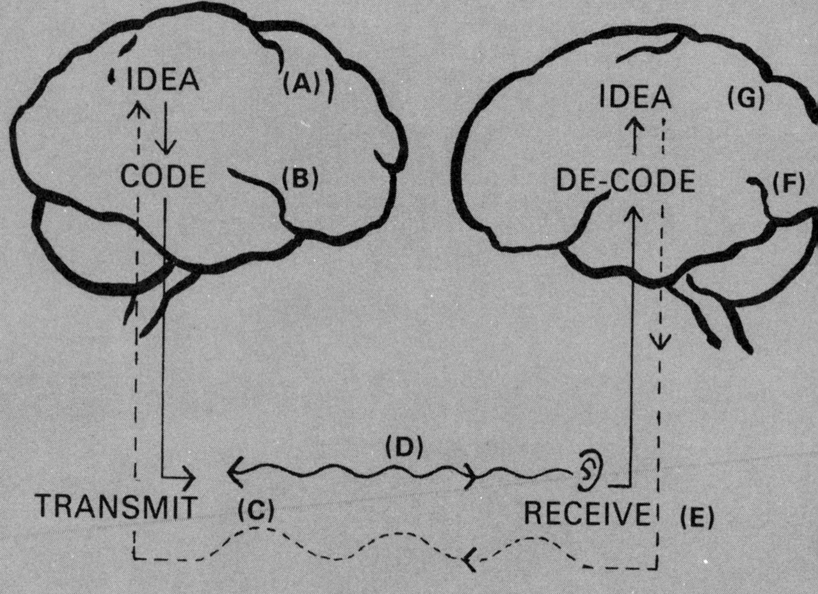

Figure 8 1. **The Communication Process.** The solid line represents the path of the original message. The idea forms in the communicator's brain (A), is translated into a code consisting of verbal and non-verbal symbols (B), is transmitted from the communicator (C), passing from one person to another (D), to be received by the receiver (E) who translates the code (F) and understands the ideas in his brain (G). The receiver then sends "feedback" by which the process is reversed – as shown by the broken line.

Chapter 8

CLOSING THE GAP

During the last months of President Lyndon Johnson's time in the White House, the term "credibility gap" was widely used, especially by those who felt that the president was not being honest about the war in Vietnam. Many people developed a suspicion that the news media, likewise, were telling only part of the truth, and there was much talk about closing the gap.

If we expect to get along with others, we must learn how to close the gap between individuals and between nations. Smooth interpersonal relations cannot exist until we have developed the ability to communicate. Everyday comments such as "I wish I could figure out what my kids are talking about . . . ," "If that preacher would just quit talking over my head," or "If only we could talk to the Russians . . . ," all point to a truth which is widely recognized: man *must* learn to communicate better.

We need more than desire if there is to be meaningful interaction between people. We must know something about the nature of communication: what it is, how it works, when it is effective, how it is hindered. This is not an easy subject to understand for communication is a very complicated process.

Consider, for example, what happens when two people attempt to communicate (see figure 8-1). First, an idea forms in the communicator's brain. This idea, if it is to be transmitted to another, must be transformed into codes or symbols. The selection of symbols depends on the communicator's education, vocabulary, intelligence, personality, attitudes, emotional feelings, and prejudgments about the person to whom the message is directed. It will also depend on what we might loosely call the communication situation. Because of situational differences, a man will use different symbols when expressing affection for his wife, giving instruction to his Sunday School class or venting anger over a buckled fender. In most conversations, verbal symbols – words – will be chosen, to be accompanied by non-verbal facial expressions, postural movements, and gestures. After all of this, the coded message goes out in the form of sounds that can be heard, actions that can be seen, or touches that can be felt. The receiver picks up these symbols, transmits them to his brain and then attempts to decode, or make sense of the message. Here again, the meaning he derives from it will depend on the receiver's education, vocabulary, intelligence, personality, attitudes, assumptions about the sender, and emotional feelings at the time. As the receiver then reacts to the message, he puts his reaction (or part of it) into code, and feeds it back to the original source. This circular process occurs quickly and continually. Before he finishes the first half of a sentence, the communicator may be getting feedback from the receiver, feedback which can alter the content and symbols used in the second half of the sentence. If the listener shows a puzzled look, for example, the communicator may make some changes in the rest of the message.

Breakdowns in communication can occur at any point in this complicated process. If a teacher is unclear in the classroom, for example, the problem may occur because the idea in the teacher's brain is not very clear in the first place, because the idea is poorly expressed (coded), because the speaker mumbles so that the idea is not clearly transmitted, because the student (receiver) does not hear the message, because the student does not understand the meaning of the words or other symbols that are being received, or because the message is misinterpreted in the student's brain. If we then apply all of this to a whole group – or a whole congregation – we can see that the opportunities for communication breakdowns are legion. It is not surprising, then, that communication is considered a complicated process and that its study has become a highly involved field with many skilled experts.

But what about the non-specialist who simply wants to get along with people? How can we communicate more effectively? To answer these questions we must build on the groundwork that has been laid in previous chapters and consider four major ingredients of communication: the communicator, the message, the channel, and the receiver.

THE COMMUNICATOR

In *Communication for the Church,* Raymond W. McLaughlin lists the characteristics of a good communicator.[1] He is a person of integrity who is morally upright. He has the courage of his convictions and says what he thinks, but he is open-minded and fair. He is an individual with a minimum of prejudice, who respects his listeners by recognizing that they are also people with opinions and ideas. The good communicator is not narrowly self-centered. He is willing to look within and to be honest about his own strengths and weaknesses. He is concerned about his physical appearance, knowledgeable about his subject matter, and willing to work to get the message across "and into somebody else."[2]

Although the Bible is not a textbook on effective communication, it says a great deal about the subject and includes some advice to the communicator. "Let your conversation be gracious as well as sensible," we read in Colossians 4:6. Our speech should be logical (Titus 2:8) and should not include backbiting (Proverbs 25:23), gossip (Proverbs 17:9, 26:20),[3] untruths (Proverbs 10:18), or evil talk (Titus 3:2, Ephesians 4:31; I Peter 2:1; James 4:11). Indeed, we should be careful of all that we say (Matthew 12:36; James 3:2) for the Scripture clearly points to the destructive power of wagging tongues (James 3:4–8) and sharp words (Proverbs 15:1).

Uncontrolled speech, expressed in the heat of anger has accentuated and sometimes caused much of the tension that divides men today. The writer of Proverbs must have recognized this when he suggested that if we were really smart, we should be inclined to keep our mouths shut (Proverbs 10:19, 17:27). But this is hard, if not impossible, for man to do by himself (James 3:8).

The way in which we communicate, therefore, like the rest of our lives, must be under the control of the Holy Spirit.

THE MESSAGE

In discussing communication, it is important to distinguish three types of messages: incidental, expressive, and goal directed. In *incidental* communication, a message is sent even though the communicator has no intention (and sometimes no knowledge) of doing this. In subtle ways, "people communicate their backgrounds, interests, wants and needs, knowledge and ignorance, and a host of other information – without having the slightest inclination of doing so, and often in spite of a definite desire for concealment."[4]

Expressive messages indicate how we feel – excited, happy, afraid, frustrated, etc. They tell something about the communicator but they often require no response from the recipient. In contrast, *goal directed* messages are designed to create some effect on the thinking or behavior of the recipient. Very often, in seeking to transmit goal directed messages, we also send expressive and incidental messages. When these three are in contrast (as is the case when we are making untrue statements while trying to "cover" our real feelings), the recipient often notices the discrepancy. Sometimes he concludes that actions speak louder than words and he ignores or rejects the goal directed message that the communicator is trying to get across.

Apparently this happened during the 1960 election

campaign in the United States. Richard Nixon reportedly believed that the voters were primarily interested in hearing the candidates discuss the issues. Eight years later, as a wiser candidate, Nixon adopted a different strategy. He accepted the counsel of his advisors and de-emphasized the issues. The advertising experts devised and sold an image in which Nixon's undesirable characteristics were glossed over and the candidate's positive traits were emphasized in attention arresting, persuasive advertising gimmicks. Apparently most of the voters got the message – largely an incidental message – which the campaigners were trying to get across: this is a "new Nixon," not the old "tricky Dick."[5]

Even when an individual attempts to communicate honestly, only a portion of what he feels or thinks will "get across." Some ideas will be transmitted through each of the three messages just described, but even then communication is limited by the available words and non-verbal symbols. If we want to be effective, we need more than the personal characteristics summarized in the preceding section. In addition we need to work at sending clearer messages.

How do we communicate a better message? First, we begin by choosing symbols which the recipient clearly understands (terms like "blessing," "redeemed" or "sanctification," for example, are meaningless to many people). We must seek to get clues into the message which will be clear to the receiver, and avoid symbols which will be confusing. Secondly, we must strive to present these symbols in a logically organized sequence with correct grammar. This is a tall order which requires more than a little effort. It is much easier to be grammatically sloppy and to use terms which the recipient only vaguely comprehends but this can and often does create misunderstanding.

All of this is not meant to imply that communication is always difficult. Sometimes it is relatively easy. When we are with people who speak our language, have had similar past experiences, hold some of our prejudices, and share our ways of looking at the world, then even poorly formulated messages are likely to be understood. This is especially true when the communicator and recipient both sincerely want to understand each other. Communication is more difficult when the message must pass between people with different cultural backgrounds, different languages, different ways of looking at things or differing definitions of the same term. Communication is also difficult when disagreeing parties bring their biased presuppositions to an interpersonal situation. At such times there are numerous opportunities for misinterpretation and misunderstanding.

Nevertheless, good interpersonal relations are only possible when we transmit clear messages. Everyone can learn to be more skillful in this task but this is especially true of Christians. Jesus taught His followers that the Holy Spirit teaches men what to say (Luke 12:12). Does it not follow, therefore, that when the Holy Spirit controls the life of a believer, he has a divine source of help in formulating his messages? Apparently, God gives greater communication gifts to some men, but all of us can still strive, under the Holy Spirit's guidance, to be better communicators.

THE CHANNEL

Information is transmitted to a receiver through various channels. Sound waves, television signals, written words, telephone wires, and a host of other media are used to extend ourselves and to send a message on to another.[6]

Usually, communication will be more effective when the sender uses several channels and when the receiver keeps as many channels open as possible. The words that are used, the inflections in the voice, gestures, facial expression and many other clues combine to give a more complete message than any one of these channels used alone. Television, for example, with its verbal and visual channels is often more effective than the "sound only" of radio. At a more personal level, if disagreements arise between people or there are threats to our self concept, it is more pleasant and convenient to "tune in" to that which supports our preconceived notions. But to get a better understanding of the true situation we must expose ourselves to more than one source (and channel) of information.

THE RECEIVER

Every communicator is, at times, also a receiver, and the characteristics of a good communicator are also necessary in the person who receives a message. The receiver must listen to what is transmitted, decode the message, detect the intent of the communicator and give appropriate feedback messages. Too often we forget that in effective communication these tasks of the receiver are as important as the work of the sender. Recently I led a group of high school students in a discussion concerning the trouble with the local church. When several of the teenagers complained about the poor sermons, I noted that these were the same young people who passed notes, giggled and flirted during the service. Little wonder that they didn't "get" anything. When a listener is disinterested in the message, inconsiderate of the communicator, only making a half-hearted attempt to listen, and more interested in talking himself, then real communication is impossible, regardless of the quality of the message or the skills of the sender. Closing the communication gap is a two sided effort.

It is possible to be spiritually alert, willing to face ourselves, secure enough to recognize our prejudices, honest before God and other men, motivated to see things from the other man's viewpoint, but unable to relate to other people because we don't listen. According to the Bible, there is a time to speak, but there are also times when we must be silent (Ecclesiastes 3:7) both in the presence of God (Matthew 26:62-3; Habbakuk 2:20; Psalm 46:10) and in the presence of other men (John 8:6; Luke 23:9).

Careful listening could well be the most difficult aspect of communication. Because of our tendency to jump to conclusions we often fail to perceive what another is trying to say. Carl Rogers, the famous psychologist, once suggested a little experiment to demonstrate this point:

> The next time you get into an argument with your wife, or your friend, or with a small group of friends, just stop the discussion for a moment and for an experiment, institute this rule. "Each person can speak up for himself only *after* he has first restated the ideas and feelings of the previous speaker accurately, and to that speaker's satisfaction." You see what this would mean. It would simply mean that before presenting your own point of view, it would be necessary for you to really achieve the other speaker's frame of reference – to understand his thoughts and feelings so well that you could summarize them for him. Sounds simple, doesn't it? But if you try it you will discover it is one of the most difficult things you have ever tried to do."[7]

A willingness to listen so carefully that you can accurately paraphrase a speaker, Rogers continues, leads to "improved communication, to greater acceptance of others and by others, and to attitudes which are more positive and more problem solving in nature. There is a decrease in defensiveness, in exaggerated statements, in evaluative and critical behavior."[8] When a disagreement is too hot for this procedure to work, a neutral third party can often summarize the views to the satisfaction of each speaker. This enables opinions to be voiced and heard without the emotional distortion generated by argument.

A sincere attempt to communicate, a careful formulation of messages, a wise use of various channels, and a willingness to listen with care – these together form the basis of good communication. Good communication, in turn, closes the gap between individuals and becomes the basis for smooth interpersonal relations.

---

[1]*Raymond W. McLaughlin,* Communication for the Church *(Grand Rapids, Michigan: Zondervan, 1968), pp. 71-73.*

[2]*In a textbook published several years ago, communication was defined as "the process of getting an idea out of you and into somebody else." It was emphasized, correctly no doubt, that a communicator is responsible not only for giving out the message, but also for insuring that the message is received and understood by one or more other people. See Eugene L. Hartley and Ruth E. Hartley,* Fundamentals of Social Psychology, *(New York: Alfred A. Knopf, 1952), p. 160.*

[3]*It is interesting to note that in a list of great sins (Romans 1:29-31), whispering (i.e. gossip) and backbiting are included along with such things as murder, fighting, and hating God.*

[4]*Robert B. Zajone,* Social Psychology: An Experimental Approach *(Belmont, California: Wadsworth Publishing Company, 1966), p. 58.*

[5]*The "selling" of political candidates is described in two interesting books:* The Selling of the President 1968, *by Joe McGinnis (New York: Trident, 1969), and* The Image Candidates: American Politics in the Age of Television, *by Gene Wyckoff (New York: Macmillan, 1968).*

[6]*See Marshall McLuhan,* Understanding Media: The Extension of Man *(New York: McGraw-Hill, 1965).*

[7]*Carl R. Rogers, "Dealing With Breakdowns in Communication," in* On Becoming a Person *(Boston: Houghton-Mifflin, 1961), p. 332.*

[8]*Ibid., p. 334.*

[9]*For an excellent summary of other barriers to communication see McLaughlin, op. cit., chapter four.*

Chapter 9

ONE SIDED EFFORTS

The preceding chapters have discussed a number of practical steps for improving interpersonal relations. We will get along better with others, it has been suggested, if we make a willing surrender to the power of the Holy Spirit; take an honest look at our own strengths and weaknesses; reject the non-involvement, manipulation and cover-up techniques by which we hide from ourselves; sincerely desire to face our prejudices; try to be honest; attempt to see issues from the other person's point of view; and make a deliberate attempt to improve communication with others. When two or more people work to apply these principles, good interpersonal relations between them are inevitable.

But what if only one person does all of this? What if we face ourselves but the other person doesn't? What if we try to see things from his point of view but he refuses to look at our perspective? What if we try to be honest but the other person refuses to be honest in return? What do we do if other people continue to cause divisions and dissension?

First, we must realize that we are not going to get along with everybody. In encouraging the Romans to "live peaceably with all men" Paul prefaced his admonition with the phrase "If possible, so far as it depends upon you, . . ." (12:18). This is a clear recognition that sometimes people simply cannot live together in harmony. Indeed, if we hope to get anything done, there are times when we must accept disagreements and divisions as a necessity. When we spend all of our energies trying to reach a consensus to everyones' satisfaction, we often slip into dead complacency. At times Paul had problems getting along (Acts 15:36-40) and so did Peter (Acts 11:2, 3). Even Jesus with His clear self understanding and perfect knowledge of others was rejected by many people. He ended His life with a bloodthirsty crowd screaming "crucify Him!"

The way in which Jesus responded to this rejection illustrates a second conclusion. Even if others refuse to cooperate, we have no justification for doing to them what they are doing to us.

It is an established principle in psychology that whenever people are frustrated, the most natural response is aggression.[1] We want to fight back and give vent to our anger. Sometimes we attack physically but more often the reaction is verbal. At times we "tell the other person off" or, much more frequently, we spread rumors and talk about him behind his back. By criticizing a person either directly or in his absence, we give a shaky boost to our own ego but this does nothing to improve interpersonal relations. Countless homes and churches have been torn asunder because frustrated people have not kept control of their tongues.

All of this is not to imply that we should ignore our anger and silently boil within.[2] When we are seething with rage, our bodies are affected physically, our spiritual usefulness declines, and there are adverse psychological changes. In intense anger, for example, we can lose control of our intellectual abilities, the size of the problem can get out of proportion, and sometimes we do not think or act rationally. There is, in addition, some value in releasing our feelings through physical activity. Periodically hitting a little golf ball around isn't such a bad idea providing that we don't take the game so seriously that this *adds* to our frustrations. Through all of this, believers must draw on the power of the Holy Spirit who enables us to be patient, kind and self-controlled (Galatians 5:22, 23).[3]

In his letter to the Romans, Paul outlines a third way of dealing with those situations in which people are unwilling to cooperate. Apparently there were individuals in the early church who were creating dissension by teaching things about Christ which were not true. These trouble makers were persuasive, but basically self-centered. The apostle's advice for dealing with such people was pretty simple: avoid them (Romans 16:17, 18).

This does not mean that we should withdraw into suburban evangelical ghettos, secure with our own little group and unconsciously wallowing in pride because we are "unspotted by the world" or untainted in our doctrine. Such behavior is sinful and disobedient to a God who told us to go into the world as witnesses. We are, however, commanded to steer clear of people who cause dissension *because of their faulty doctrine* (Romans 16:17; 2 Thessalonians 3:6).

Faulty doctrine always results when we wander away

from the teachings of the Bible. For Christians, this departure can sometimes be so subtle that we don't even realize what is happening. Before long the stage is set for divisions and strained interpersonal relations (Romans 16:17).

There are at least five ways in which we slowly move away from the Scriptures and hence away from each other.[4]

1. Sometimes we get distracted by an interest in our personal fame and future. As a result, we compromise our position (Titus 1:9-11). We stop serving Christ and spend our energies instead in a self-centered struggle for personal gain.

2. Sometimes we become overly impressed with personalities. Like the church at Corinth (I Corinthians 3: 4-9) we split into parties and rally around some charismatic leader who, like Paul, may be appalled at this idol worship. Even in present-day evangelical circles, many church members have deviated from their God-given purpose and devoted themselves to furthering the cause of some personality.

3. At times there is division because we are distracted by concern over status. With a host of shaky rationalizations, we exclude people whose clothes, skin color, or manner of speech are different from ours. This was apparently causing dissension among believers when James wrote his epistle and stated, in essence, that the church is not to be a status-conscious "closed" country club (James 2:1-9). Rather it is to be a group of believers who

are scattered throughout the world as Christ's ambassadors (Acts 8:1-4; II Corinthians 5:20).

4. In other churches, there is division because Christians have allowed themselves to become lethargic and their ministry to become irrelevant. Too often we are like the Israelite army which David must have found when he went to visit his brothers (I Samuel 17). Doubtless these soldiers periodically put on their finest armor and marched in review. Perhaps they heard challenges about the Goliath that must be defeated, but then they retreated in fear and dismay back to their tents until the next parade. All too often, church members today dress up for a rallying call on Sunday mornings, soak up the truths of Scripture, sing "Onward Christian Soldiers" and contribute to foreign missions, but then retreat to other things, ignoring the scriptural commandments to witness to a needy world at our doorstep. Little wonder that we are surprised and uncomfortable when someone dares to challenge us because we seem to have faith but no action.

5. Then, there is the departure from the Scriptures which comes from laziness. Often we just don't bother to think about the truths which we have learned, and soon they are forgotten (Jude 17). Before long we begin to squabble with others.

All of these departures from Scripture lead to increased strife between people. They must be avoided if we want to get along with others.

But how do we avoid such dangers? How do we remain faithful to the Word of God and able – as much as possible – to relate effectively to others? The answer to these questions brings us back to our starting point: to a realization of the Holy Spirit's influence in interpersonal relations. He enables us to look at ourselves and to respect others; He teaches us to communicate; He keeps us from the faulty doctrine which divides; and He makes it possible for men of good will to live together in peace and harmony.

---

[1]*This theory was first proposed many years ago following a series of animal studies at Yale University. See J. Dollard, N. E. Miller, L. W. Doob, O. H. Mowrer, and R. R. Sears,* Frustration and Aggression *(New Haven, Conn.: Yale University Press, 1939).*

[2]*Mark 3:5 mentions the anger of Jesus. We see it expressed in John 2:13-16 and Matthew 23. In Gal. 2:11 we see Peter and Paul involved in an angry exchange.*

[3]*See Kenneth S. Wuest,* Word Studies: Ephesians and Colossians in the Greek New Testament *(Grand Rapids: Eerdmans, 1953), pp. 113-114, and Norman V. Hope, "How to be Good – and Mad,"* Christianity Today, *12, (July 19, 1968), 3-5.*

[4]*Much of the outline which follows is adapted with permission from a sermon preached by Rev. William Hadeen, Jr. at Calvary Baptist Church, Mundelein, Illinois.*